HOW TO
PLAN YOUR 'TOTAL' ESTATE
WITH A WILL & LIVING WILL

WITHOUT THE LAWYER'S FEES

By Benji O. Anosike, B.B.A., M.A., Ph.D.

3ʳᵈ, Revised Edition

Copyright © 2005 by Benji O. Anosike

Library of Congress Cataloging-in-Publication Data

Anosike, Benji O.
  How to plan your 'total' estate with a will & living will, without the lawyer's
fees : the American will kit, usable in all 50 states / by Benji O. Anosike.-- 3rd
rev. ed.
       p. cm.
  Includes bibliographical references and index.
  ISBN 0-932704-75-1
 1. Wills--United States--Popular works. 2. Right to die--United States--Popular
works. 3. Power of attorney--United States--Popular works. 4. Estate planning--
United States--Popular works. I. Title: Plan your 'total estate with a will & living
will. II. Title.
  KF755.Z9A435 2005
  346.7305'4--dc22

D1279499

Printed in the United States of America
ISBN: 0-932704-75-1
Library of Congress Catalog Number:

Published by:
Do-It-Yourself Legal Publishers
27 Edgerton Terrace
East Orange, NJ 07017

CREDITS:

Cover design, art direction, typesetting and illustration, by Amy R. Feigenbaum and Suzanne Feigenbaum of Rivanne Advertising Creative Desktop Publishing Services, Brooklyn, N.Y.

Other Books By The Author:

On Estate Planning:
- *How To Probate, Administer & Settle An Estate Yourself, Without The Lawyer's Fees*
- *How To Properly Plan Your 'Total' Estate With A Living Trust, Without The Lawyer's Fees*

On Other Subjects:
- *How To Form Your Own Profit Or Non-Profit Corporation Without A Lawyer*
- *How To Buy Or Sell Your Own Home Without A Lawyer Or Broker*
- *How To File Chapter 11 Business Bankruptcy Without A Lawyer*
- *How To Settle Your Own Auto Accident Claims Without A Lawyer*

Dedication

This Book is Lovingly Dedicated to...

Ezinne Ndiem Anosike

...thank you, Ezie, for being so loving and caring to your daddy...for literally saving and sustaining your daddy's life. Oh yes. You've made it all more than worthwhile for me!

Selfhelper Law Update Service

The laws governing the creation of Wills, Living Wills, Powers of Attorney, and other related estate planning instruments addressed in this manual, as well as the forms and formal procedures for using them, can and do change every now and then. Fortunately for us, this does not happen very often. Nevertheless, this necessitates at least two things: first, that a book such as this be revised and updated as frequently as possible, and, secondly, that readers as well as publishers be vigilant, always on the look out for possible significant changes that might occur.

We'll appreciate your assistance in helping us keep track of, and up with, this task. ***If you should come across any "local" or other form(s) or procedure(s) that are particular to your state or county or locality, or any that are new or significantly different from the ones provided in this manual, we'll like to know about it. Simply send us a written note specifying the law or procedure, and/or enclosing a blank copy of the form(s).*** Such material will be of valuable help to us in any subsequent editions and future updates and revisions. However, in addition to that, The Do-It-Yourself Legal Publishers researchers will further research into the matter and send you instructions on the new law or the use of the material, where necessary or specifically requested by the reader.

The Selfhelper Law Update Service Response Form

TO: The Do-It-Yourself Legal Publishers, **27 Edgarton Terrace, EAST ORANGE, NJ 07017** .

Dear Publisher ,

Here's the information you invited in your HOW TO PLAN YOUR 'TOTAL' ESTATE WITH A WILL & LIVING WILL, as follows *(check applicable paragraphs & add details)*:

☐ I find that the laws/procedures/forms* for my county/state* seem to have changed (to be significantly different) from the one(s) in the book in the following ways:_____
_____
_____

☐ Copy of the new or different form(s) is/are hereby enclosed.

My Name is:_____Address:_____

_____Zip_____

Phone No. (   )_____

IMPORTANT: Please do NOT rip out the page. Consider others! Just make a photocopy and send that!

_____

*Cross out the inapplicable terms or words

FOREWORD:
THE PUBLISHER'S MESSAGE

To All Our Dear Readers:

True, it's not often that one finds a legal document which is nearly as useful or beneficial as most lawyers (and judges) would claim they are. But we've found there are a few real exceptions. A valid Will is one such exception. ***IT'S SAFE TO SAY THIS ABOUT A WILL: quite easily, it is probably one of the most important legal documents that any property owner, big or small, makes during his or her lifetime!!***

The Epidemics Of Dying Without Leaving A Will In America!

It's somewhat strange, though. It turns out that Wills are the one essential legal document most Americans frequently neglect to leave behind. And don't think it's just the poor or the "dumb" that are guilty of this. Would you believe that ***President Abraham Lincoln,*** himself a brilliant lawyer, among other things, was in this company!? And so were Spain's ***Pablo Picasso,*** America's ***billionaire Howard Hughes,*** and the State of Illinois' Supreme Court Justice James Dooley, just to name a few more recent famous examples! One survey reported in the New York Times of March 30th 1978, showed that about 7 out of every 10 Americans who die each year do so without leaving a Will. The number of male intestacies (male persons who die without leaving a Will) is great. But, even then, that number is, by far, surpassed by female intestacies. Unless she possesses great wealth of her own, the average woman just doesn't think about making a Will. And her husband doesn't either.

Look, The Costs Of The Alternative Could Be Incalculable!

Yet, probably no other oversight could be more costly to one's hard-earned property or to the loved ones one leaves behind. The "costs" of not leaving a Will come in several ways: the real possibility of one's estate going to the wrong or unintended person, or to the right person in the wrong amounts; the possibility of the wrong person being appointed to serve as the "guardian" of the minor children or to manage the property the minors are to inherit; greater inconvenience, legal complications, and extra expenses associated with prolonged "probate" proceedings (in court costs, guardian fees, administrator and attorney fees, etc.); increased possibility of family disagreements and court battles, and so on.

Spain's world-famous artistic genius, ***Pablo Picasso,*** died in 1973 at the age of 91, leaving behind numerous potential heirs, and an estate valued 3 years later at $260 million. He also left behind what one 1980 writer called "the ordeal of Picasso's heirs." He had left no Will! So, even years and decades after his death, the thoughts and lives of those he left behind continued to be dominated by problems brought about by Picasso's neglect to leave a Will. Locked into countless court battles ever since, Picasso's heirs have handed one of the longest running financial gold mines to successions of art appraisers, accountants, court-appointed administrators, and lawyers hired to sort out who is entitled to which Picasso's paintings, graphics, sculptures, or ceramics. ***With a good Will, he could have easily spelt out all that. He could have easily saved everyone the trouble — and the staggering additional expenses. But since he left none, he, in effect, left it to others to make the "Will" for him.*** OTHERS HAD TO DECIDE THESE MOST IMPORTANT QUESTIONS FOR HIM: Who were to be his heirs? Which works of art should be classified as part of his estate? Who should inherit them and in what amounts? Who would coordinate and manage the affairs of his estate? Which work of art should be sold, and which should be donated to a museum, if any? By whom? Where? How? Is reproduction permissible, and if so, who should own the rights? From which part of the estate should the estate debts or taxes be paid? And so on and on.

Table Of Contents

CHAPTER 1
INTRODUCTION: THE WILL & THE LIVING WILL AS TWO ESSENTIAL TOOLS IN A "TOTAL" ESTATE PLAN SCHEME

CHAPTER 2
LET'S GET THE BACKGROUND INFORMATION STRAIGHT, FIRST: THE WILL BASICS

CHAPTER 7
HOW TO MAKE YOUR WILL CHALLENGE-PROOF IN PROBATE: THE "PITFALLS" TO AVOID IN DRAFTING YOUR WILL

CHAPTER 8
YOUR WILL AND ESTATE TAXES: IS SO-CALLED 'TAX PLANNING' REALLY RELEVANT FOR YOU IN MAKING YOUR WILL?

APPENDICES

A. MINIMUM LEGAL REQUIREMENTS FOR A VALID WILL IN EACH OF THE 50 STATES, PUERTO RICO, AND THE DISTRICT OF COLUMBIA

B. A SEPARATE LETTER (MEMO) OF INSTRUCTIONS & INFORMATION YOU SHOULD LEAVE ALONGSIDE YOUR WILL (An illustrative sample)

C. STATUTORY AND OTHER LIVING WILL FORMS FOR ALL 50 STATES

These are all the gravest of matters for Picasso's survivors. As grave as you can imagine. Yet, they don't even begin to compare with the underlying passions and bitterness which Picasso's failure to leave a Will had brought about among these surviving members of his family. Years and years of court battles, and the end never seemed to be in sight!?

Ever heard of the famous story of the man (a person of modest means) whose wife died without a Will, leaving him to share the property which had once been his home with the wife's niece? The problem? This was a niece the husband never saw eye to eye with! They had been bitter enemies. The wife's failure to make a Will had cost the husband that much — the only main property he was left with, plus emotional agitation, and embarrassment!!

The point should be obvious and there's no need belaboring it. IT'S A POINT WE CAN'T EVER EMPHASIZE ENOUGH: *whether you are young or old, a millionaire or a pauper, whoever you are, so long as you care for the well-being of your family and some loved ones, one thing you can't afford to live — or die — without is a good Will. Yes. You just can't. And neither can your family or loved ones!!*

What's Behind The Widespread Failure By Americans To Have A Will?

An interesting question is: why is it that so many Americans fail to make a Will? Richard Phalon, a New York Times writer, estimates that one reason is that, being human, we generally "don't like to contemplate our mortality." Another reason is that most of us are procrastinators by habit — we put off making a Will again and again to some time "soon". Maybe not tomorrow, but soon.

But beyond these factors, there are two real "biggies" which account for the common attitude about Will-making among the public: the absence of commonly accessible medium of public education about the vital necessity for estate planning in general, and leaving a Will, in particular; and the good, old problem of not being able to afford the high attorney fees and elaborate redtapes traditionally associated with drawing up a Will.

How This Book Is Meant to Lick The No-Will Epidemic

This manual is one practical answer. It's basic objectives are simple: **i)** to take the legalistic mystique out of Will-making by providing the ordinary man and woman the essential information; and **ii)** to commonize the use of Wills in every household by making it practical for the average person to make and afford one.

The manual can easily serve the common needs of 90 or 95 per cent of all American adults in each of the 50 states. ***But a word of caution is called for:*** *You must read through it, every word of every chapter, from the beginning to the end, to gain the widest possible insight into the essence of what is involved. Do not just glance through or hastily skim around the manual!*

Indeed the good news is: the evidence is growing that, like the millions of American homeowners or drivers who have long chosen to take wrenches, hammers and screwdrivers in hand to escape the trademan's or the mechanic's high fees, the consumer of legal services is now beginning to "do it himself," especially in the area of Will-making. Tom Goldstein, the New York Times legal affairs reporter, reported this result of a survey commissioned by the American Bar Association: "At least for now, lawyers enjoy near monopoly (79%) in the drafting of Wills...But it (i.e., the survey) also tentatively identified a trend that fewer people are using lawyers for drafting Wills."[1]

With this manual in hand, almost every American who wants to have a Will (and a 'Living' Will) can easily do so — competently, simply, and inexpensively. *To be sure, nowadays there is no shortage of books (and even computer programs) on "estate planning" and on Wills and Living Wills. In deed, it can even be said, rather, that nowadays there is a proliferation and a super-abundance of it, rather than a shortage. FINDING ONE, THOUGH, THAT IS AS COMPLETE, COMPREHENSIVE, COMPETENT, AND UNDERSTANDABLE TO THE ORDINARY MAN OR WOMAN IN THE STREET AS THIS VOLUME, IS THE REAL PROBLEM!*

Thank you very much.
Do-It-Yourself Legal Publishers

---

[1]Quoted from The New York Times, Feb. 22, 1978, p.C.9.

HOW TO USE THIS MANUAL

A few words about the use of this guidebook. The "heart and soul" of this book—for a reader, especially, who is primarily concerned with actually writing his or her own Will or other similar estate planning instruments—are **Chapters 4 & 5.** These two chapters deal with what could aptly be described as the "nuts and bolts" of Will drafting—the actual process of practically doing it.

But, as you are quickly reminded by the manual (Section D of Chapter 1), if you are to have a sound overall estate plan, the Will should only be employed within a "complete"' or "total" estate plan concept; as just ONE essential instrument among a handfull of related but equally essential instruments which must, as well, be employed in one's estate plan to complement and supplement the Will. In light of that, **Chapter 6** could be viewed as something of a "secondary" nuts and bolts chapter; it addresses the drafting and signing of the related instruments that should (MUST!) go with a Will in any modern-day "total" estate planning scheme—*the Living Will, the Medical Directive, and the Durable Financial and Medical Power of Attorney.*

However, before one can effectively undertake the actual drafting of any of these instruments, one would need to have had certain basic knowledge and information: about the essential law and requirements, about the major issues that need to be addressed, the necessary legal and technical procedures for going about it, etc.—matters which are addressed elsewhere in other chapters.

Thus, **Chapter 2** deals with the estate planning needs and objectives for which a Will (and other devices) are employed, and the fate that you and your loved ones stand to suffer if you were to fail to have one. **Chapter 3** deals with going about the task of data-gathering on one's personal affairs and possessions as a basis and prelude for the drafting of the instruments. **Chapter 7** addresses a vital question, the tiny bits and pieces of different procedural and technical measures you'll need to build into your Will document—the major "pitfalls" to avoid—in order to ensure not only that the instruments will stand up in court, but that it will be virtually challenge-proof. And, Appendix A spells out the essential legal requirements for a valid Will in all 50 states and other jurisdictions in the nation. And so on and so forth.

Granted, Chapters 4 & 5 (and, similarly, Chapter 6) are the most pivotal segment, as these sections lay out a systematic, step-by-step procedure for properly drafting and "executing" a valid Will and other related instruments, and finally weaves the whole process into a "total" or "complete" estate plan scheme. But, as you will quickly discover in reading through or using the guidebook, for you to be able to properly and actually draw up the stated legal instruments under Chapters 4 & 5 and 6, you need to have first mastered the background materials—materials which are contained elsewhere in the manual, in the other passages alluded to above.

SO THE ADVICE IS THIS: first of all, to begin with, read and comprehend all the "background" chapters—*Chapters 1 to 3,* and **7 *and* 8,** and *Appendices A, D & E,* to name just a few. Then, finally, go to the chapters that tie it all together for you, first to *Chapters 4 & 5,* and SYSTEMATICALLY AND ORDERLY follow the procedures outlined therein to work out and sign a valid Will. Then, in accordance with the book's prescription of the "total" estate plan approach, go next to **Chapter 6,** and, following the step-by-step procedures outlined therein, also crank out the *Living Will, the Medical Directives,* and the other essential supporting documents.

A lot of times, you would probably not need all or some of the information provided in a given chapter; some information may be irrelevant or inapplicable in your particular situation. It's all here, though, just in case you need it!

Chapter 1
INTRODUCTION: THE WILL & THE LIVING WILL AS TWO ESSENTIAL TOOLS IN A "TOTAL" ESTATE PLAN SCHEME

A. THE PURPOSE OR PURPOSES OF ESTATE PLANNING

In today's financial and social environment the art of *"estate planning"* — the planning for the efficient management of your "estate" (meaning the wealth and property you accumulated in your lifetime) during your lifetime, as well as for its proper transfer or deposition, including providing for your loved ones, after your death — is almost universally viewed by experts as a vital component in any sound and overall financial and retirement planning. This phenomenon has assumed an increasingly special place especially in this era, owing to longer life expectancies and medical breakthroughs.

For our purposes in this manual, suffice it simple to say that, for a variety of objective reasons, financial planners and financial and legal advisors increasingly see the need for all persons, young and old alike, rich as well as poor, to "plan" their estates. For one thing, *good estate planning will, at the very least, provide you a framework by which to assess your estate and to also gain its optimum enjoyment during your lifetime. And, perhaps most importantly, estate planning, if done well and timely undertaken, will help bring one critical fact clearly home to you: the very need for you to plan your estate, and the stark reality that if you fail or neglect to do so, the government will do it for you any way, like it or not!*

B. IN THE FIELD OF ESTATE PLANNING DIFFERENT DEVICES ARE USED TO ACHIEVE DIFFERENT OBJECTIVES

In point of fact, the term *"estate planning"* is a catch-all term for describing a range of objectives from which to choose, and the use of different tools and devices with which to accomplish them. *Among the most common estate planning objectives for most people, are the following:*

1. Avoiding "probate" — which, in essence, really means avoidance of an often horrendous array of court costs and expenses, and the lawyers fees and long delays involved in probating an estate [See Appendix E for more on the probate process].
2. Minimizing death taxes {See Chapter 8 for more on estate taxation].
3. Arranging for proper distribution of your property, and for proper care, guidance and maintenance of your minor children and loved ones, if you should die.
4. Determination of what is to be done and choosing who is to make the important legal, financial and medical decisions, or to handle your affairs, if you should become incapacitated.
5. Planning for your funeral and final settlement of your estate and affairs.

C. THE PARTICULAR ESTATE PLANNING TOOLS & DEVICES CONSIDERED IN THIS MANUAL

As mentioned above, in practice, the way the 'planning' process is basically done is that particular devices are used to attain particular estate planning objectives, in terms of one's objectives and needs. For example, LIVING TRUSTS are a device primarily used for probate avoidance; certain gift-giving schemes, on the other hand, are devices used for estate tax reduction or minimization.

The subject matter with which this manual is primarily concerned — namely, the Will, the Living Will, and the Financial and Medical Durable Powers of Attorney — is primarily concerned with the 3rd, 4th and 5th estate planning objectives outlined above, namely, providing for the proper disposition of one's property and affairs after death; the proper care, guidance and maintenance of one's minor children and loved ones; determination of one's major health care and financial affairs if one should become incapacitated, and general directives on one's burial and funeral.

More specifically, the following are the vital estate planning tools addressed in this manual:
   i) The Will
   ii) The Living Will
   iii) The Durable Financial Power of Attorney
   iv) The Durable Medical Power of Attorney with a Medical Directive Component

1. The Will

Virtually all financial planning experts are agreed that the Will is a fundamental, even indispensable corner-stone of any sound estate planning. In deed, virtually all are agreed that probably no other tool in estate planning quite accomplishes the basic role of a Will as well as the Will does, namely: the planned disposition and distribution of a decedent's property and settlement of some deep personal affairs, such as funeral and burial preferences. And all are agreed that, whatever other tools or techniques one may have in one's estate plan, the Will should almost always be employed as one of the tools to complement and supplement such other tools or techniques to make for a sound and "complete" estate plan.

One major reason this is so is summed up by Benjamin T. White, an Atlanta lawyer and estate planner, even as he noted that in recent years, revocable living trusts have been marketed by many experts as something of a substitute and a superior alternative to Wills: "It's virtually impossible to get all of your assets into the trusts. [Nor can you use a trust to name a guardian for your children]."[1]

Perhaps this will clear it up for you. THE EASIEST WAY TO UNDERSTAND THE DIFFERENCE IS PROBABLY THIS. FIRST AND FOREMOST, UNDERSTAND WHAT A WILL DOES, WHAT IS ITS MAIN FUNCTION: *a Will settles and disposes of the assets and other personal affairs you hold in your name. In other words, it is concerned with that category of assets that will just have to go through the probate process — the so-called "probate assets."*

The second category of assets, those that do not go through the probate process (the so-called "non probate assets"), do not get disposed of by a Will, but would "pass directly" to your heirs by "operation of law" — e.g., assets held jointly with another person, life insurance proceeds, assets held in trust, Individual Retirement Accounts and other retirement benefits, and the like. (See Appendix D, at pp. 107-9, for examples of this category of assets.)

One recent report on the question put it rather sharply this way:

> "[One common misconception these days is that] if you have a trust, you don't need a Will. Wrong. You should have a Will even if you put all your assets into a trust set up deliberately to distribute your property outside of probate. A Will can insure that assets not covered in your trust document (a last minute inheritance or money won in a lottery or lawsuit) get into the trust. Finally, a Will can take care of such other matters as naming a guardian for minor children."[2]

In sum, the point is that just about every tool in the estate planning arsenal is specialized and limited in what it can do, and none can substitute for or do what a Will does. Hence, if you are to have a "total" or complete estate plan, the better estate planning strategy is to have a good Will, as well as other appropriate estate planning devices to complement it—the Living Trusts, Living Wills, Durable Power of Attorney, etc.

2. The Living Will

The "LIVING WILL" is a relatively new legal document which, along with such related documents as The DURABLE POWER OF ATTORNEY, THE MEDICAL POWER OF ATTORNEY, and the like, has assumed an increasing significance as a vital estate planning tool in recent times with the growing reality of longer life expectancies and continued medical breakthroughs among the population.

---

[1]"When 'Living Trusts' Makes Sense: Tackling The Dreaded W-Word," NY Times, Sunday, Nov. 11, 1990, Business Section, p. 17.

[2]Theresa Meehan Rudy, et al., How To Use Trusts To Avoid Probate & Taxes (Random House., 1992) p. 7.

One report aptly defines the Living Will this way:

> "The written declaration of a wish not to be treated for a terminal illness. Frequently it is characterized as the 'pull the plug' Will. The purpose of a Living Will is to give a person the right to determine the nature of his or her death ... [and it's role is primarily to spell out] the individual's right to [give] advance directives regarding the stopping of life-sustaining procedures that would only 'prolong artificially the dying process.' "[3]

The Living Will is frequently mentioned in the same breath as the regular Will. In Chapter 6 we provide details on the drafting of this increasingly important estate planning instrument.

3. Durable Financial Power of Attorney & Medical Power of Attorney

A Durable Power of Attorney is also a relatively new legal document in the field of estate planning. In a word, the **Durable Financial Power of Attorney** is a document which designates an agent or person (he's often called a "proxy" or an "attorney-in-fact") to make <u>financial</u> type of decisions for you if you should become incapacitated to make such decisions, by reason of mental or physical defect; the **Durable Medical Power of Attorney,** on the other hand, is a document which similarly designates an agent to make <u>medical</u> or <u>health care</u> types of decisions for you under similar circumstances. An integral part of the Durable Medical Power of Attorney is what is known as the **"Medical Directive,"** which basically spells out some specific medical actions, procedures or treatments that should be taken in specific or representative situations of mental incompetence or incapacitation for further guidance for all interested parties so that all parties (your appointed proxy, the doctors, family members, etc) will have a more specific and definite idea of what you would want in given or representative situations. In both cases mentioned above, the instrument is effective and operational ONLY DURING the period, if any, when the person making it is mentally and/or physically incapacitated.

The Durable Power of Attorney (whether it is of the financial and/or of the medical kind) is generally intended to be used in conjunction with a LIVING WILL. In deed, many financial planners today say that these newer family of instruments are today just as important as the traditional Will.

We provide in Chapter 6 the details concerning the drawing up of these newer family of instruments.

Wills seem basic, but most people die without them.

A Helping Hand

A durable power of attorney allows someone to take care of such financial choices as:

- Paying your bills
- Buying and selling your securities
- Cashing checks
- Selling your house
- Opening or closing bank and brokerage accounts
- Collecting money due you

---

[3]Irving J. Sloan, Wills & Trusts (Oceans Publications, 1992) p. 145.

D. SUMMARY: COMBINING THESE TOOLS IN A "TOTAL" OR "COMPLETE" ESTATE PLAN SCHEME

By way of a summary, here are the central points of this chapter to bear in mind:

1. Given at least that any good estate plan must have as one of it's objectives the proper disposition of one's property and affairs in it's entirety, after death, a regular Will will almost always have a place as a useful tool in any estate plan.
2. Once a Will is drawn up, however, the Living Will should not be far behind and should just as well be drawn up.
3. But a Living Will is incomplete unless it is backed up and complimented by two other instruments — the Durable Financial & Medical Power of Attorney, and the Medical Directive.

In other words, as an estate planner, the plan you devise should be considered within a "complete" estate plan concept along the lines suggested above — a plan that aims at assembling all of the component parts essential to the given estate plan goal you have in mind. Your estate plan should, in short, almost always contain the Will, as well as the Living Will, the Durable Financial and Medical Power of Attorney, and the Medical Directive!

This is the basic approach taken in this manual — the Will (and other related legal instruments) as ONE essential piece in an overall "complete" estate plan configuration. And, for <u>YOU</u>, the estate planner or estate plan-designer, as you go about reading through this instructional manual and, hopefully, drafting your will and/or other estate planning instruments, you are well advised to bear this central principle in mind—ALWAYS.

Documents to appoint a health care proxy are as important as a will.

Preparing for Ill Health

Common terms in health care planning.

Living will: Stipulates the type of treatment desired should you be unable to make your own decisions.

Health care proxy: A person designated to make health care decisions for you if you become incapacitated.

Durable power of attorney for health care: Designates an agent or proxy to make health care decisions.

Medical directive: General terms for documents that provide direction on the type of care you desire.

Chapter 2
LET'S GET THE BACKGROUND INFORMATION STRAIGHT, FIRST: THE WILL BASICS

A. WHAT IS A WILL?

A Will is a special statement made by someone, usually in writing,[1] by which he or she gives instructions on how his or her assets, property, and debts, should be distributed or otherwise disposed of, and his spouse and children taken care of, AFTER his (or her) death. *To be acceptable as legally valid, however, the document has to be drawn up and signed according to certain specific rules set down by law of the state of one's permanent residence.* (See Appendix A for a summary of the requirements of each of the 50 states for a valid Will.)

B. WHAT DOES A WILL DO FOR YOU?

To sum it all up in one sentence, the fundamental thing a Will does for you is this: it makes it as probable as anyone can legally make it, that if and when you die, the property and loved ones you leave behind would be distributed or looked after strictly according to your own wishes rather than somebody else's. To say it differently, a good Will pretty much assures you that your hard-earned property and loved ones would not fall into the wrong hands, or into the hands of someone or institution you might not have intended or preferred.

C. WHAT ARE THE ADVANTAGES OF LEAVING A WILL?

The following are the major advantages of having a Will:

1. If a person dies without leaving a Will (called dying "intestate" in legal jargon), his (or her) property would automatically pass to relatives according to the formula set down by the laws of "Descent and Distribution" of the particular state. The state, in effect, writes his "Will" for him and dictates how and in what amounts his property is to be distributed!

Does one's surviving spouse receive everything one leaves behind when there is no Will? No. In most states (Alabama, Alaska, Arizona, California, Colorado, Florida, Illinois, Massachusetts, Michigan, New Jersey, and New York, if only one child surviving, are among them), the surviving spouse is only entitled to one-half of the estate and the other one-half goes to the child or children to share equally. In many other states, though fewer in number (e.g., Arkansas, Ohio, South Carolina, South Dakota, Tennessee), the surviving spouse gets one-third and the other two-thirds goes to the child or children. To put it briefly, if you have children, it's guaranteed that each and every one of them will share with your spouse — including your children by a former marriage who may have been self-supporting or self-sufficient adults!! (There have been known cases where spouses were reduced to literally begging for assistance from their children in no-Will situations. Indeed, in a state like Delaware, for example, the spouse has a right only to live in the family home — for just her lifetime. Every other real property, plus the rest of the personal property (except $50,000) goes to the children to be divided up by them!)

Suppose, however, you have no children and you die intestate, would your spouse now be entitled to everything? No. She (or he) gets her one-half (or one-third or other share, as the case may be), and your surviving parents, brothers and sisters will share the balance. But suppose you have no close relative at all? Then, says the no-Will law formulas of most states, your property goes to your next closest living relations — a distant cousin, the child of a deceased aunt or uncle, and what have you. That may be all well and good with you. But wait a minute! What if it turns out that this very relative is the most hated snub you ever knew or wished to

---

[1]Certain special types of Wills are unwritten. See Section I of this Chapter.

leave anything? Or, what if you would have preferred to leave everything to your spouse, or to her and only some of your children? Then that's just too bad. Nobody can do a thing about it now.

(The tables on pp. 10 and 11, Figures 2-A & 2-B respectively, present an illustration of how two states, Florida and New York, distribute property in no-Will situations.)

2. The "penalties" for not leaving a Will are even more severe when one is survived by minor children. For one thing, the court will step in and select persons of its choice to be the ***"guardian"***[2] of the minor's "person" when, with a Will, you would have been the one to select the person of your choice, say your parents or trusted relative, to act as the guardian; or you could even have provided that no separate guardian of the minor's "property" (as differentiated from his "person") should be required. The guardian does not work for free — he gets a fat fee, taken out of the minor's property.

3. With a Will, it's YOU that picks who is to serve as the ***"executor"*** of your estate — that is, the person or persons who are to manage what you left behind and see to it that your wishes are carried out. YOU pick and choose anyone you prefer. In the absence of a Will, the court — and NOT you — would have to make that appointment, and the person it appoints may be that irresponsible child or unfaithful spouse of yours. Or, it could even be a total stranger altogether!!

4. Now, suppose that for whatever reason you wanted to favor one particular relative or family member over another; or that you wanted to leave some (or all) of your property to a particular relative, or to that close friend of yours who may have cared for you during your last illness? Or, suppose you wanted to leave a particular item of special economic or sentimental value to a specific person; or you wanted to make a special gift to a favorite charity, church or organization? How do you accomplish this? A Will is just about the only comprehensive, catch-all instrument (or at least one of very few such instruments) by which you can do this.[3] In sum, without a Will you can't make special provisions for special persons in your life.

5. Having a Will saves your estate a lot of money. How? It's simple: with a valid Will and a good overall estate plan, you are better able to hold down the cost of managing your estate (the "administration" costs) just by the fact of having a properly drawn Will. Here's how: in a no-Will situation the person who the court appoints to administer or take care of your estate (the ***"administrator"***) would have to be running back and forth to the court for permission to carry out most of his important functions. He may have to first get the court's permission to sell estate property, or to pay bills and expenses; he may be required by the court to hire an accountant, lawyer or property appraiser; and he would probably have to take out a "bond" (an insurance) designed to protect the heirs and creditors of the estate. And here's where it hurts: all these activities, known as "probate procedures" in legal parlance, are not simply offered free of charge. Not at all! Indeed, they are frequently very expensive, usually cutting very heavily into the value of what is left of your property. Monies, in the thousands and millions of dollars, are frequently wasted away that way, with known cases, especially in modest-sized estates, where the whole estate was totally exhausted!

If, on the other hand, you made a Will and appointed an Executor, say, your spouse or a trusted relative, to administer the estate, he or she will usually serve without pay and the unnecessary administrative costs are almost totally eliminated. No bond would also be required, providing you so provide in your Will.

6. You've probably heard of the term "estate planning"? This has to do, simply, with the whole business of planning and managing what one owns or acquires in such a manner as to retain as much of it as possible during, and as well as after, one's lifetime. Well, having a good Will is thought of by most financial experts as one of the essential and most important aspects of sound estate planning. One reason this is so is because a properly drafted Will enables the maker to plan and organize his/her overall affairs and estate much better. This way,

---

[2]NOTE that the law requires that any property inherited by underage persons shall be managed on the minors' behalf by an adult until they come of age.

[3]Of course, there are the so-called Will "substitutes" — jointly held property, life insurance policies, revocable trusts, etc. (See Appendix D). But almost all of such substitutes are usually used to supplement rather than substitute for a Will, as explained in Appendix D of the manual.

upon the death of a person, his/her loved ones are left with something of a clear road map and far less confusion and agony to contend with.

D. SHOULD YOU ALWAYS HAVE A WILL?

The answer is emphatically YES. Always. From all the advantages gone over in Section C above, it should be obvious that a Will is a very essential thing for every thinking adult to have — whether rich or poor, married or single, old or young. And for all the advantages, all it would take are a few hours of one's time.

E. SUPPOSE YOU HAVE ALL YOUR PROPERTY IN JOINT NAMES & TRUSTS. IS A WILL STILL NECESSARY FOR YOU?

The question often posed, not only by neophytes in estate planning, but also by persons of relative sophistication in financial matters, goes something like this: "I already have all our property in trust and the rest of it jointly in my wife's (husband's) name and mine, and we own pretty little anyway. So, do we still need a Will?"

The answer, it turns out, is a resounding YES! The plain truth is that even with the best estate plan in the world, there's still a need for a will; there's no escaping it — by and large it's simply a cornerstone you must have if you are to have a sound, overall estate plan!! The only thing that may be different is that if the estate plan you otherwise have is really that good, the will you'll need will merely be a simple one (something like a **"back-up" or "pour over" type of Will** for a person with a good Living Trust, for example). But you should still have one — and need to have one — all the same.

True, if you have your property in an instrument like a Living Trust, that property will pass directly to the designated beneficiaries and will not have to go through the hated "probate" process. And, true, you can put your property into any number of "non probate asset" forms which, again, will make such property ineligible to go through the probate process — forms such as jointly held property, life insurance proceeds, U.S. bonds, payable-on-death bank accounts, etc. But you'll never be able (nobody can) to get all of the assets you have into a trust, or into the non-probate asset types of assets! Nor, will you be able to use a trust or any other devices to do certain other things that a Will can do for you, such as to name a guardian for your minor or dependent children. IN OTHER WORDS, A WILL WOULD ALMOST ALWAYS BE STILL NEEDED TO TAKE CARE OF THOSE ASSETS YOU MIGHT HAVE OVERLOOKED, OR THAT INEVITABLY WOULD BE LEFT OUT OF A TRUST AND OTHER SIMILAR PROBATE-AVOIDANCE MECHANISMS, OR TO TAKE CARE OF OTHER AFFAIRS, FINANCIAL AS WELL AS NON-FINANCIAL, IN YOUR LIFE.

Here are some of the situations that make it necessary to almost always have a Will, regardless:
- Only with a Will can you distribute or otherwise dispose of property you might have somehow excluded or overlooked in your trust or other probate-avoidance devices — for example, newly acquired property or property acquired in the future for which ownership or title transfer papers have not been completed; property you might come to inherit or acquire by gift; alimony award; lottery winnings, etc.
- Only with a Will can you designate a personal guardian to look after the care and upbringing of your minor or dependent children, if you have any; and with a Will you can appoint a property guardian, as a "back up" guardian, to preserve and manage any property left for the children, even if a provision to that effect has been made in a children's trust.
- Only with a Will can you designate a person (an "executor" or a "personal representative") who can administer and represent your "total" estate and affairs in a comprehensive, overall manner. That is, an executor is in a position to represent your total estate, to deal with anything and everything of significance concerning you, your property and your affairs with anybody and everybody — disposition of property, care and maintenance of the spouse or children or other relatives, funeral and burial arrangements, the inheritance of a child or spouse, forgiveness or payment of debts, etc...
- With a Will you can designate who you want your "residuary estate" (property not specifically allotted to anyone) to go to, or what specific assets you want used to pay estate taxes or debts assessed to your estate.
- See also Appendix D (pp. 107-9), esp. Section C therein, for more on this issue.

F. WHO INHERITS YOUR PROPERTY IF YOU DIE WITHOUT A WILL?

When a person dies without leaving a Will (called dying "intestate" in legal jargon), the laws of Descent and Distribution[4] (same thing as the law of "Intestate Succession") take over and become the controlling formula by which his or her estate is distributed. Each state has specific rules about the persons or classes of people entitled to inherit under conditions of intestacy. The Intestacy Succession laws of the state where the decedent was permanently domiciled at the time of his death would govern. However, as a general rule, some persons who bear certain relationship to a decedent are almost always entitled to inherit from him or her under the laws of just about every state.[5] *They are, in their order of priority, the following:*

1. THE SPOUSE

With a few rare exceptions — such as where a spouse has waived his or her rights of inheritance under a separation or antenuptial agreement, or where he/she had been found guilty of adultery, desertion or failure to support the other spouse — the surviving spouse may not be totally disinherited by a decedent spouse, but has a primary right to a share of the decedent's estate. This right, called the spousal "right of election" in legal jargon, is said to belong to each spouse *"by affinity"* of the marital relationship, as opposed to a relationship by blood. In more recent times, some courts have ruled, though, that even if the spouse or heir is cruel to the deceased, that will not prevent the heir from inheriting from the estate, nor will the conduct of the heir have any bearing on the size of the share that he or she will receive, except for just one situation: when the spouse or heir murders the deceased. In such a situation, the Murder-Beneficiary Rule will apply and the beneficiary loses any right to inherit.

In addition to the normal distributive inheritance share of the spouse, the laws of most states also provide for a "family allowance" in money and property to be set aside for the support and maintenance of the surviving spouse and children until the estate is eventually distributed — specified household items or funds from the estate, the family home or apartment, and the like, depending on the particular state.

2. LINEAR DESCENDANTS

Next to the surviving spouse, come that class of the descendant's heirs who would inherit by virtue of "direct" (also called "linear") blood line. This is the class of people with the closest blood relationship to a decedent, according to law and custom. This group includes the decedent's children, grandchildren, and parents, in that order. Generally, the children and their descendants take a set proportion of the estate along with the spouse. (When children survive their parent, grandchildren do not, as a group, share in the grandparent's estate; grandchildrenwould be entitled to inherit from the grandparent's estate only if their parent was entitled to share in the estate but was deceased without getting the share.)

Note that in almost all the states, illegitimate or adopted children are considered "blood" relatives, and that half-blood relatives in most states are entitled to inherit equally with those of whole blood.

In the following states, if a married person dies intestate and with no lineal descendants (children, grandchildren, etc.), the entire estate goes to the spouse: Arizona, Arkansas (unless marriage lasted less than 3 years), Colorado, Florida, Georgia, Illinois, Kansas, Mississippi, Montana, Ohio, Oregon, Tennessee, Virginia, West Virginia and Wisconsin. This remains applicable even where the spouse was no longer living with the decedent at the time of death, and the deceased was survived by needy parents. In the remaining states, the property is divided between the spouse and the deceased's parents under such a situation. If there are no surviving parents, then the whole property goes to the spouse.

3. LINEAR ANCESTORS

Linear ancestors are the decedent's parents, if surviving. They may generally inherit in situations where the decedent leaves no surviving spouse, children or their ancestors. [See Figure 2-C in p. 12 for illustration].

---

[4]See Figures 2-A and 2-B at pp. 10 and 11 for a detailed breakdown of the way property is distributed in the states of Florida and New York under no-Will situations.
[5]Ibid.

4. THE COLLATERAL KINDRED

Collateral kindred are such relatives of the decedent as his or her brothers and sisters or their descendants, or, where it becomes necessary, other so-called "next-of-kin" persons still further removed from the decedent, such as the uncles, aunts, nephews and nieces, first cousins, and the like.

5. FINALLY, THE STATE

Now, just what happens to a decedent's property when there's no known or available relative to inherit his property under the state laws of inheritance? It's simple: the law says that such property *"ESCHEATS"* — that is, it automatically passes to the state.

Figure 2-A

FORMULA FOR FLORIDA'S PROPERTY DISTRIBUTION TO
DECEDENT'S HEIRS IN ABSENCE OF WILL

FIGURE 1
CHART OF INTESTATE SUCCESSION

A Man Dies Leaving	If No Will His Property Goes To	His Wife	His Only Child	His Children	His Grand-children	His Parent or Parents	His Brothers and Sisters
Wife and one child		Half	Half				
Wife and two children		One-third		Two-thirds			
Wife and four children		One-fifth		Four-fifths			
Wife, one child and two grand-children (children of deceased child)		One-third	One-third		One-third		
Wife and parents, but no children or grandchildren		All					
One or more children, but no wife				All			
Parents and Brothers and sisters; no wife, children or grandchildren						All	
Brothers and sisters, but no wife, children, grandchildren or parents							All
No immediate family	*See Section 731.23, Florida Statutes*						

Figure 2-B

FORMULA FOR NEW YORK'S PROPERTY DISTRIBUTION
TO DECEDENT'S HEIRS IN ABSENCE OF WILL

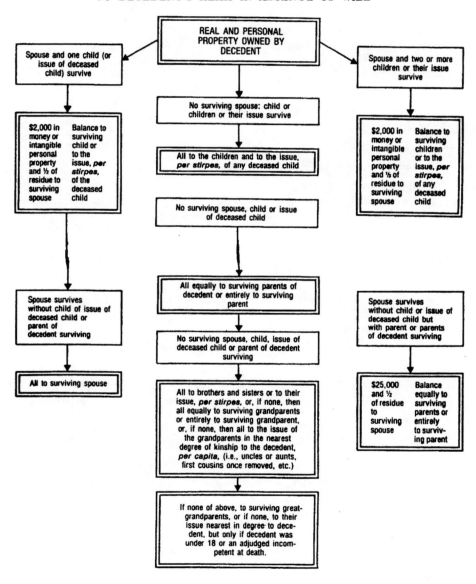

Figure 2-C
General Succession Of Heirs In Intestate Distribution Situations:
Distribution Based On Family Relationships

The following illustrates the general order of priority by which one's assets will be distributed to his or her relatives, when there is no surviving wife or children. (For the specific pattern of succession distribution and the related percentages, refer to the probate code of the given state).

Explanation:

① Distribution would first be to the parents (if living); if not living, then distribution would be to the brothers and sisters ②; if neither the parents nor the brothers or sisters are living, then it will go to the nieces and nephews ③, if any are living, and so on.

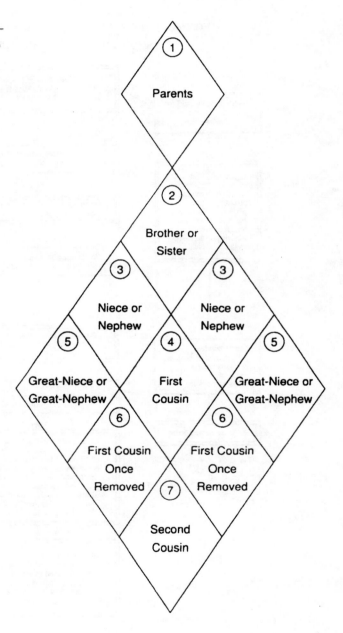

G. SOME COMMON MYTHS ABOUT WILLS

The following are some of the most common myths which often prevent many from making a Will, or make them put it off till it's too late:

1. *That only the rich or persons with considerable amount of property need to have a Will.* This is not true. On the contrary, it is just as essential for the less well-off to have a Will as it is for the well-off: one man's fortune is often another man's shoeshine money. And further, a Will doesn't just distribute property; it also provides for the guardianship of children, tax and probate savings strategies for the estate, burial preferences of individuals, and other important personal and family matters like that.

2. *That a husband and wife who have their property in "both names" have no need for a Will* since such property would automatically go to the surviving spouse any way. This is not quite accurate. The truth is that even when a husband and wife have all their major property in joint names with the "right of survivorship" provision, it would still be beneficial for them to have a good, well-coordinated Will made up. For example: say you own a house which you put in both names giving each spouse the right to the house in the event of the death of the other. There are still other eventualities you could not have provided for or possibly anticipated except by a Will. What if, for example, the two spouses were to die at the same time, say in a common plane or auto accident? And so on and so forth. The possible scenarios are simply infinite.

   Then there's another kind of problem with this thinking. A tax problem: without the special tax advantages available through a good Will, an estate which falls within the "large estate" category ($675,000 and over for deaths occuring in 2000 or thereafter) would likely suffer some higher tax consequences.

3. *That once you make a Will, it means your days in the world are numbered;* hence it is better to wait until your old age (till "later") before making a Will. This is, of course, pure superstition that makes no sense whatsoever. The fact that one makes a Will today, or waits till a hundred years from now (if one gets that far, of course!), has nothing to do whatsoever with how long one lives. Indeed, as an aside, the sooner one makes a Will, the better. Don't put it off till you are forced by some sudden emergency to have to make one under conditions of stress, hurry or illness.

4. *That a Will is final, fixed and permanent.* Another myth is that because a Will carries such an authoritarian-sounding title as the "Last Will and Testament" of the maker, *it is final and can't be changed once drawn up and signed.* False. The truth is that you may change your Will even as often as once a day—if you want to.

5. Another erroneous belief shared by many is the idea that any expression of wishes or intentions made orally or in a letter can serve as a Will. False. It can't. To be acceptable as a valid Will, the letter (or oral expression) would have to be a most unusual one which meets all the minimum requirements for a valid Will (Appendix A) as they apply to the given state where the decedent permanently resided.

6. Finally, there is the belief that the holding of property by a couple under "joint names" automatically saves the estate from estate taxes upon the death of either or both partners. Not quite so. Under the current tax law taking effect from just 1981, a jointly held property is not taxable to a legally married partner who survives the other, anyway. However, upon the death of the second spouse, such property is 100 percent taxable to her (the second spouse's) estate —whether held in joint name or not. Furthermore, there may be tax disadvantages related to "capital gains" taxes on such property.

H. SHOULD YOU REVISE OR AMEND YOUR WILL OFTEN?

Yes, you should. Everyone with a Will should make it a duty to review it as often as every two or three years, depending on the flow of events in one's life. Wills which are not up-to-date at the time of the testator's death are often a source of problems and court fights among family members or beneficiaries.

Also, aside from the fact that it is always a good idea, in and of itself, to review your Will periodically to ensure that it reflects the changing needs and circumstances, there's one further important recent reason why this might be necessary: to take into account the recent changes called for by the 1981 tax law (See Chapter 8). In general, Wills and estate plans written before the 1981 tax law featured two basic kinds of trusts for the surviving spouse — 1) the type designed to qualify within the maximum marital deduction permissible under the previous law (no more than $250,000 or one-half of the taxable estate, whichever was larger); and 2) the so-called "qualified life interest" type of trust, which was designed to pay "income" to the spouse, allowing her to live off the assets of the estate for the rest of her life and allowing the estate to avoid death taxes when she (the second spouse) died, at which point the heirs inherited the trust assets.

Generally, if your Will was written before the effective date of the present tax law (September 12, 1981), and it established trusts as the primary vehicle for reasons of minimizing federal estate taxes, it should be reviewed and revised to reflect the new higher exemption levels for estates. Further, people should now review their asset holdings and the size of their assets, anyway. While the use of trusts will probably continue to be advisable for couples with larger size estates (estates worth $675,000 or more), the use of such devices in one's Will may altogether be unnecessary for couples whose combined estate's size does not approach or exceed $675,000, the current maximum federal exemption level. And, of course, the use of trust formats will in any event continue to be necessary for people using trusts for reasons other than reducing taxes — such as to avoid probate or to reduce the amount of an estate subject to probate, for example.

Revision of a person's Will is called for particularly when there is a change in his or her circumstances. Events which may indicate that an existing Will needs to be changed or updated would include the following: new parenthood or grandparenthood by the testator, divorce, changes in the needs of the beneficiaries, change of residence, sale or disposal of property mentioned in the Will, death or absence of an executor, trustee or beneficiary, acquisition of new assets, and a drastic fluctuation in the value of the estate. (Procedures for amending a Will by use of Codicils and otherwise, are set forth at p. 39-40).

I. THE THREE BASIC TYPES OF WILL:

There are three basic types of Wills. They are:

Type 1 - *The Regular or Statutory Will.* This is a Will which is written up and signed in the normal, deliberative course of things — that is, after the maker has taken time to think things out in a calm, deliberate state of affairs. The two main elements that differentiate this type of Will are: i) it is a written, not oral statement which follows the statutory requirements stipulated by the given state for a valid Will; and ii) it is not made under an unusual circumstance or in time of an emergency, as in Types 2 or 3 below.

Type 2 - *The Holographic or Olographic Will.* This is a Will which is written up and signed by the maker only, and in his or her own handwriting. (As a practical matter, this type of Will is mostly usable in situations involving soldiers, sailors, and merchant marines in active service. And to be acceptable as valid, it must also meet certain specific conditions given by each of the 25 states which recognize holographic Wills, as set forth in Appendix A.)

Type 3 - *The Nuncupative Will.* This is an "oral" Will — that is, one that is made by an oral declaration, rather than in writing. Usually, such Wills are acceptable only under certain special circumstances, such as when the maker is in imminent danger of death from illness or extreme emergency from which he subsequently dies as a direct result of that specific danger. To be acceptable as valid for Will purposes, the oral declaration has to have been made under these conditions: i) before eye witnesses; and ii) the oral statements must subsequently be put in writing by a witness within a few days or so after the declaration was made.

J. WHICH OF THE THREE TYPES OF WILL IS BEST FOR ONE TO USE?

Most estate plan experts would almost always advise you to use the Type I Will. (Unless, of course, one's circumstances make that strictly impossible.) Certainly, it is the most ideal or desirable type for one to use from a planning standpoint. The reason this is so is this: The Regular or Statutory Will is the one that allows the maker the maximum opportunity to plan, assemble, and sort out the totality of his affairs in an atmosphere of calm deliberation and lack of pressure, and to declare his intentions in an unmistakable way — in writing signed by him before two or more witnesses. Because it is usually done in a cool, more calculating, deliberative manner, the Type I Will is generally considered to be the most credible of the three, the least subject to fraud, undue influence or manipulation by dishonest persons or relatives.

K. SOME DON'TS: CERTAIN THINGS A WILL CAN'T DO FOR YOU.

There are certain things a Will cannot do or be used for and should therefore be generally avoided. *They are:*

1. Legally married spouses generally can't be disinherited from certain types of or all of their marital property, even if the Will provides otherwise. (There are a few states which exempt personal property from this rule.) A similar rule generally applies as well where there has been a legal separation (but not a divorce) between the couple. In such instances, the "innocent spouse" — that is, the one who obtained the separation decree or agreement against the other — may still inherit the normal spousal share of the marital property, no matter what the Will says.

2. A Will cannot usually disinherit a partner from gaining total ownership of a property that is jointly or mutually owned by the parties under the "right of survivorship" provision.

3. With the exception of a few states where it may be otherwise, those stipulations in a Will which totally disinherit the testator's family and donate everything to the church or to charity is usually unenforceable. At least in part. The children — but not the spouse — may often be disinherited by such a provision, provided they are of legal majority age and are expressly mentioned in the Will. (There is no legal obligation for anyone to leave relatives of a lesser relationship anything.)

4. A stipulation in a Will leaving money or property to a corporation is unenforceable UNLESS the corporate charter of that corporation expressly authorizes such gifts as permissible.

5. Generally, the terms and provisions in a life insurance policy concerning the beneficiary of the insurance proceeds are the controlling terms. And if a Will should provide otherwise, the terms of the Will would be disregarded. The same thing applies also to the U.S. Government Savings Bonds or to pension rights.

6. A stipulation in a Will which requires a beneficiary to engage in an act of illegality or immorality as a condition for being entitled to the gift is not enforceable.

7. Where a couple lives (or owns property in) a *"community property" state,* all property acquired by either the husband or the wife DURING the time they were married, belongs to both spouses in EQUAL shares. And since each spouse, in effect, already owns half of the estate, obviously neither can disinherit the other in that half which is already his or hers. (The nine community property states in the nation are: Arizona, California, Idaho, Louisiana, Nevada, New Mexico, Texas, Washington and Wisconsin.)

8. In planning to make a Will, you may, if you like, consider making a *"mutual" Will* — that is, two separate Wills by married couples in which each spouse makes similar or reciprocal provisions concerning the beneficiaries and the executor or executrix. However, as a general rule, it is frequently advisable to avoid making a *"joint" Will* — that is, a single document signed by both spouses together. It is usually better and simpler for each spouse to have a separate Will; the probate procedures of joint Wills could be needlessly complicated on the death of the second spouse, especially if he or she dies in a state other than where the Will was first probated for the first spouse.

L. CAN A LAY PERSON PROPERLY MAKE HIS OR HER OWN WILL WITHOUT A LAWYER?

The answer is YES, YES, YES! For a number of reasons: First of all, get this basic fact into your head right away: there is nothing in the laws and regulations of any state governing Wills which says that only a lawyer should — or can — draw up a Will. Nothing at all! Quite to the contrary. The simple fact is that anybody whatsoever, whether he or she be a lawyer, a mailman, a garbageman, a doctor, or what have you, has the legal right to draw up his or her own Will.

The second point is this: the correctness or legal validity of a Will (or, for that matter, any legal document or contract of whatever kind) does not in any way depend on what the maker's professional calling or title is. The fact is that in general, ANY WILL DRAWN UP AND SIGNED BY YOU, THE NON-LAWYER (OR ANYBODY ELSE), IS JUST AS LEGALLY VALID AS ONE THAT MIGHT HAVE BEEN PREPARED BY THE WORLD'S BEST LAWYER — *as long as it meets certain basic tests of clarity, inclusiveness and propriety and complies with the legal requirements set down by the testator's state for a valid Will. The profession or title of the person who makes it up has absolutely nothing to do with it!*[6]

The third point, which is just as important, is this: After all is said and done, there's really one — and only one — underlying objective for which a Will is made, and that is to express THE MAKER'S OWN intentions. It is the maker's intentions, not a lawyer's or any body else's intentions, that a Will is meant to express or reflect. (Indeed, even when you hire a lawyer and pay him to draw up your Will for you, it will still be left to you, the testator, to tell him what you want him to put in your Will!) Now, you are, after all, the only one who knows your family needs better than anyone else; you are the one who knows exactly how you feel and how you would like to see these needs met or provided for. So then, why hand it over to another human being, even one who bears some awesome-sounding title, to express your own intentions for you — for a fat fee?

Of course, we do not mean to say that every non-lawyer can (or should) necessarily draw up his or her own Will. Not at all. In truth, there are certain persons who either cannot or should not undertake that task themselves — such as lunatics, incompetents, or persons with unusually large or complex estates. (See Section M below.) Persons of this kind would fall within the category of people who legitimately ought to use the help of a lawyer — a competent lawyer who knows what he's doing. Fortunately, though, it turns out that the number of people who would come under this category is very very small — less than 5 per cent of the relevant American population, according to current informed estimates!!

M. COULD YOU POSSIBLY HAVE A PROBLEM MAKING YOUR OWN WILL?

This is the "acid test" right here. If you don't have any of the following rare, personal problems in your particular circumstances, you may easily draw up your own Will without any problem:

1. If you don't have an "ante-nuptial contract" existing between you and your spouse. (An ante-nuptial contract is a contract or agreement signed by you and your spouse before your marriage as to the property rights of each of you.)

NOTE: If an ante-nuptial contract or agreement does exist in your situation, or if you have a valid Separation Agreement or decree from your spouse, then all you have to do is to make sure you carefully read those sections in the agreement under the headings, "Inheritance Rights," "Release," or "Waiver of Election Rights," and proceed to write your Will accordingly — that is, only making sure that the provisions in your Will are consistent with the provisions of the marital agreement.

2. If you don't lack legal "competence" to draw up a Will. (That is, a physical or mental ability or fitness to adequately do or know what you are doing; for example, one who suffers from conditions like insanity or underage, or is extremely old and feeble.)

---

[6]Indeed, one experienced and widely respected lawyer, Boulder Colorado's Harper Hamilton, has called it "a great myth in our society that one must have a lawyer to prepare a Will" — a characterization that is widely shared among disinterested experts. "Must a lawyer be hired to prepare a Will?" asks attorney Edward E. Colby of California, the author of Everything You've Always Wanted to Know About the Law. "No, any person can prepare his own will if that is his desire....... If you think you are knowledgeable..... there is no law that makes it mandatory to hire a lawyer to prepare your will ..."

3. If you do not have more than one marriage with children in each marriage, especially if you can see a probability that conflicting claims would develop among your spouses and children after you're gone. (In general, if there are no children from the prior marriages, or if you are fully divorced from all the previous spouses, then there shouldn't be much of a problem here; this will still be true whether you have remarried or not.)

4. If your total estate is not worth in excess of $675,000 , which is the threshold above which your estate becomes possibly subject to an estate tax liability. (Only the top 1 percent or so of income earners and property owners in the United States generally meet this particular requirement, by the way!) [See Chap. 8, at pp. 65-74].

How did you do in the above test? As you would probably figure out from the above criteria, it is not too often that one comes across persons who have the kind of "problems" that are serious enough to render them incapable of writing their own Wills! And if you have none of these, you can go right ahead with your Will-making, assured that you can come up with a finished document just as good as — or even better than — what any lawyer can give you.

READY? When you are ready to actually draw up your Will, turn to Chapter 4 for the step-by-step instructions on how to prepare and draw up your Will.

Chapter 3
GATHERING THE ESTATE FACTS & INFORMATION IN PREPARATION FOR DRAFTING THE WILL: THE WORKSHEET

This WORKSHEET is meant to serve two prime purposes. First, it should be used for the purpose of gathering and assembling vital information together in preparation for the drafting of your Will or Trust and as an aid in your overall estate planning process. And, second, it is to serve as a personal affairs record of essential basic information to assist the Executor of your Will and/or the Administrator of your estate, in having all of the information he or she should need to better carry out his duties.

The worksheet should be updated frequently to keep it current almost always, and a current copy should always be kept alongside your Will as it will be a great help to the executor of the estate in the settling of the estate or other similar emergency.

𝕿𝖍𝖊 𝕰𝖘𝖙𝖆𝖙𝖊 𝕴𝖓𝖋𝖔𝖗𝖒𝖆𝖙𝖎𝖔𝖓 𝖂𝖔𝖗𝖐𝖘𝖍𝖊𝖊𝖙

FAMILY INFORMATION

1. Your legal name in full: _____
2. Other names by which known: _____
3. Date of birth _____ Place of birth _____
4. Social Security Number: _____
5. Spouse's name: _____
6. Spouse's date of birth _____ Spouse's place of birth _____
7. Spouse's Social Security Number: _____
8. Home address: _____
9. Business address: _____
10. Place and date of present marriage: _____
11. Prior marriages: (date and place of marriage and how it was terminated:)
12. Name(s) of former spouse(s): _____

CHILDREN (by birth or adoption) by present marriage:

13.	Name	Date of birth	Address

Grandchildren:

14.	Name	Date of birth	Address

OTHER RELATIVES

15. Parents: Of Yours   Of Your Spouse's

Father's name and age: _____

Address: _____

Living ☐   Deceased ☐   Living ☐   Deceased ☐

Mother's name and age: _____

Address: _____

Living ☐   Deceased ☐   Living ☐   Deceased ☐

16. Other relatives (included in Will). [Your brothers, sisters, grandparents, aunts, uncles, nieces, nephews, etc.]
_____

17. Special medical or financial needs or conditions of self, spouse and dependents, if any: _____
_____

INSURANCE
18. List all insurance policies, pensions, life, retirement & death benefits:
    Type of policy & Company   Policy number
_____
_____
_____

19. Accounts & Notes Receivable: _____

BUSINESS INTERESTS AND AGREEMENTS
20. List all business interests and affiliations you're currently involved with and any business agreements that you are a party to:
_____
_____

STOCKS, BONDS, CD'S, SECURITIES, ETC.
21. Description & Location   Date acquired   Original cost
_____
_____
_____

22. **ADVISORS** (Give name, address, and phone numbers):
    Family doctor: _____
    Clergy: _____
    Attorney: _____
    Financial advisor: _____
    Stock broker: _____
    Insurance agent: _____
    Banker: _____
    Accountant: _____
    Trustee of trusts: _____
    Alternative trustee: _____
    Executor(s) & Alternative(s): _____
    Guardian(s) & Alternative(s): _____

23. **RECORDS**
    Indicate the EXACT location of the following records:
    Birth Certificate _____
    Family records: _____
    Military records: _____
    Will, Living Will, Power of Attorney, etc. (originals): _____
    Corporation/Partnership records: _____
    Trust documents: _____
    Stock certificates, bonds, etc...: _____
    Retirement and pension records: _____
    Safe deposit box and key: _____
    Bank book and savings passbook(s): _____
    Insurance policies, etc...: _____
    Property/Real estate deeds and titles: _____
    Powers of attorney: _____
    Prior federal tax returns: _____
    Automobile titles: _____
    Gift tax records: _____
    Medical records: _____
    Cemetary deeds: _____
    Funeral home information: _____

Your Social Security Card: ———————————————

Spouse's Social Security Card: ———————————————

Promissory notes: ———————————————

Divorce Papers from Prior Marriages: ———————————————

Postnuptial/Antenuptial agreements: ———————————————

Credit card records: ———————————————

Club, union, civic or fraternal organizations: ———————————————

BANKING

24. *Checking accounts, savings accounts, etc...*

Institution (Name & Address)	Account type & how held (Joint, survivorship, trust, custodial)	Account numbers

REAL PROPERTY

25. *List all interests in real properties:*

Type of property	Location	Interest owned, estimated value, mortages

AUTOMOBILES

26. *List all interests in automobiles:*

Type	License number	Insurance Co.

OTHER PERSONAL PROPERTY

27. List major items of personal property owned (including furs, jewelery, art, cash on hand, all items of substantial value):

Description of item	Location

28. Safe deposit box (Location and under what name registered): ———————————————

29. Other investments: (nature and in what names held) ———————————————

30. Liabilities: (Notes and loans payable, accounts payable, mortgages payable, taxes due, credit card accounts, real estate taxes, etc...)

31. Miscellaneous Information:

FINANCIAL STATEMENT   Date when last revised:_____

Suggestion: Complete this section in pencil so that changes can be made from time to time as necessary.

A. List Your Assets

Real Estate (land, home, business property, condos, co-ops, etc.)
Description or address   Type of ownership (sole, joint, etc.)   Market Value Equity
_____
_____
_____

Cash or Equivalent Funds (checking accounts, savings accounts, money market accounts, certificates of deposit, etc.)
Bank   Account Type & number   Balance
_____
_____
_____

Investments (stocks, bonds, mutual fund shares, CDs, other securities, etc.)
Type   Company   Number of shares   Market Value
_____
_____
_____

Personal Property—whatever you own (furnitures, clothes, etc.) that are not major. (You need not list individual items unless of significant value)
Description   Approx. value
_____
_____
_____

Automobiles—List all interests in automobiles
Type   License number   Insurance Company
_____
_____
_____

Retirement Plans (IRAs, profit sharing, pension plans, Keoghs, etc.)
Type   Name of plan   Beneficiary   Current value
_____
_____
_____

Life Insurance (also note the policy number and type of insurance coverage, such as "whole" or "term")
Insured Person   Company   1st Beneficiary   2nd Beneficiary   Death Benefit
_____
_____

Accounts/Notes Receivable & Debts owed you (include name, address and phone number)
Who owes   Amount owed
_____
_____
_____

Special items of value (items of substantial value, e.g., coin collections, antiques, jewelry, art, etc.)
Description   Approx. value
_____
_____
_____

B. List Your Liabilities

Type   Company/Persons Owed   Amount owed   When due   Secured by

Mortgages

Installment Loans (credit cards, etc.)

Education loans

Personal loans

Taxes owed

Other debts

C. Figuring Out Your Net Worth

AMOUNTS

Husband   Wife   Joint

ASSETS

Real Estate
Cash or Equivalent Funds
Investments
Personal Property
Automobiles
Retirement Plans
Life Insurance
Accounts Rec./Debts owed to you
Special items of value
Deferred compensation (income earned but not received)
Total Assets.................................. (A)

LIABILITIES

Mortgages
Installment Loans
Education loans
Personal loans
Taxes owed
Other debts

Total Liabilities................. (B)

NET ESTATE.............................
(assets minus liabilities)

(A) — (B)

Major assets not in the Will, if any

Jointly-Owned Property: List all property or assets, whether included in the above Assets & Liabilities schedule or not, which are not in the will but are jointly owned and can thus be transferred automatically to the other owner. (Describe each form of joint-property ownership concerned—real estate, bank accounts, stocks and bonds, etc.)

1. Type of Property: _____

    Address of property or by whom kept: _____
_____
_____

2. Type of Property: _____

    Address of property or by whom kept: _____
_____
_____

3. Type of Property: _____

    Address of property or by whom kept: _____
_____
_____

Chapter **4**

LET'S DRAW UP THE WILL: STEP-BY-STEP PROCEDURES

A. SOME HELPFUL PROCEDURES FOR WORKING OUT A GOOD WILL

1. Before you start the actual writing of the will itself, you should first sit down in a calm, quiet place, with your pen in hand and think. JUST THINK FOR A MOMENT. Run down, in general terms, the whole range of provisions you would want to make in your Will — for your wife or husband, children, relatives, friends, etc., as the case may be. Jot down the ideas as you go along.

2. Assemble in your mind — as well as on a written list — the assets you own or have an interest in, and the debts owed to you; then the debts and obligations you owe to others. And if you have forgiven (or wish to forgive) any of the debts anyone owes you, make a note of it so that you can enter it in your Will. [Use the ESTATE INFORMATION WORKSHEET on pp. 18-23 to help you in orderly assembling your assets, liabilities, records etc...]. *In deed, this is usually the very starting point for estate plan professionals in the practical drawing up of a Will (or trust): the inventory and evaluation of your estate for an overall idea of what you own, owe, etc.!*

3. If you have already made significant gifts separately to a beneficiary you also plan to name in your Will, make a note of it. That fact should be clearly specified in the Will, and should also be coordinated and made compatible with the provisions of the Will and the Trust, and other estate plan instruments, as applicable.

4. Is there any extraordinary circumstances in your personal or family situation — e.g., a prior marriage that has not been completely and legally terminated, children by a prior marriage, stepchildren or adopted children, illegitimate children for which you are responsible, and the like? If there are, do not just merely lump every body together under general terms like "my children" or "my wife". You must generally specify which particular children (or spouse) you refer to in each instance by his/her specific name.

NOTE: Note that there are several ways by which one can "own" property; and that property owned in a particular way is treated in a particular manner on the owner's death. *The most common popular ownership forms are as follows:* **i)** individual or "sole" ownership, usually evidenced by being registered only in one name (this is the most basic ownership form); **ii)** "joint tenancy" or "tenancy by entirety" (shown usually by being registered in the names of both husband and wife, and when the first party dies, the surviving party owns the whole thing); **iii)** "tenancy-in-common" (ownership by two or more parties who are not marital partners; each party owns equal proportional share only); **iv)** "partnership," when two or more persons own property together pursuant to a written (or oral) agreement, usually more applicable in business deals [when one partner dies, the "partnership" is often dissolved and the deceased partner's particular share of the assets is considered part of his/her estate]; and **v)** "community" property, a form of marital partnership wherein all property obtained during the parties' marriage, except any acquired by gift or inheritance, is "community property" — i.e., belonging equally to both spouses. With respect to community property, upon the death of one spouse, the surviving spouse is entitled to only his/her one-half of the community property assets. (Property owned prior to marriage and property received solely by one spouse as result of a gift or inheritance, is the separate property of that spouse.) The 9 community property states in the nation are: AZ, CA, ID, LA, NV, NM, TX, WA, and WI.

5. Make sure you clearly describe and identify any property or asset, real or personal, assigned to persons in the Will, in such a manner that there can be no misunderstanding whatsoever later about your exact intentions or which items in particular you have in mind.

6. In general, be simple and clear in the language of your Will. (Avoid the usual legalese the lawyers love to use in writing Wills, such as "I give, bequeath, and devise...," when you could simply say, "I give ..." and still mean EXACTLY the same thing but with less confusion.)

7. In drawing up the Will, allow for the unexpected and for different contingencies if there could be an abnormal occurrence. For example, remember that while most wives often die after their husbands, and most children after their parents, it doesn't always happen that way.

8. Allow for the possibility of there being a contest over the terms of your Will — depending on your particular circumstances.

9. As much as possible, try to avoid having in your Will any of the "dont's" specified in Section K of Chapter 2 (p. 15), and the classic "pitfalls" in Will-drafting specified in Chapter 7 (pp. 61-4).

10. Bear in mind that it is important for a wife to have a Will as it is for a husband (even if the wife has little or no property of her own), and vice versa. In line with this, you and your wife or husband may want to make a "mutual Will," that is, two separate Wills whose provisions are similar or reciprocal. If so, just make sure that you expressly specify whether the provisions of the Wills are to be revocable by the surviving spouse, or to be absolutely irrevocable. (Irrevocability provision usually becomes relevant where one or both spouses has reason to believe that the survivor will give his/her inherited property to a future husband or wife. However, you should also note the fact that where a binding agreement to leave property to a third party exists, the bequest to a spouse won't qualify for the "marital deduction" allowance for estate tax purposes.[1])

11. NOTE clearly that as to the contents of the Will, you do NOT have to specifically itemize in the Will each and every one or all of your property—say the stocks and bonds, and their policy numbers, the name of your broker, the exact address of where you bank and who you have savings accounts with, details about your pension and profit-sharing benefits, your car, real estate, and so forth. In fact, it's an unwise procedure to do so, since that will warrant that any time you change or add to your holdings, however slightly, you'll have to totally change or amend the Will! THE BEST WAY TO HANDLE THAT IS THIS: Make a separate memo (handwritten or typed), listing all such detailed information therein [see Appendix B, *"Letter or Memo of Instructions and Information,"* on pp. 79-84 for a sample]. Keep this memo always attached to the Will to inform your executor on the details of the issues.

12. Bear in mind that, in all probability, as a practical matter, the only time you'll probably need to worry about ever having a "tax problem" in making your Will, would be if you happen to be one of those few persons in society fortunate enough to have a far more-than-average-sized estate. (See Chapter 8 for more on estate tax fundamentals before you conclude your Will-drafting).

B. THE ACTUAL DRAFTING OF THE WILL

Now, we come to the actual drawing up of the Will.

To prepare the Will, here's the first thing you need to do: understand what your state's legal requirements are for having a valid Will. To do this, ask yourself: in what state do I maintain my permanent residence? Then turn to Appendix A on p. 75 of the manual for the requirements as they relate to your particular state. Bear such requirements strictly in mind as you go about the process of drawing up the Will.

NOW, in the next few pages, you will find: **1)** the _**PRACTICE**_ **Worksheets** for the Will drafting starting from p. 32; and **2)** the **numbered _INSTRUCTIONS_** starting from pp. 26-31, which tell you how to complete the practice sheets and what to fill in in the spaces provided.

You may first make a photocopy of the PRACTICE worksheets and use these for your Will drafting work. Then, fill out the Practice worksheets <u>first</u>, following the numbered instructions that start from p. 26. You should go just one step (and only one step) at a time, starting from the beginning. Do not skip around from page to page. Fill in the appropriate information in all the Practice worksheets, from the first page to the last, and as you go along, cross out those paragraphs (or terms or provisions) which do not apply to your particular situation, if any. (On p. 31 you're instructed on how to type up the final copies of the Will, after you shall have completed the drafting.)

---

[1]See Chapter 8 for estate tax fundamentals.

ATTENTION: *You May Want To Order The Standard Will Forms.*

Legal stationery stores generally carry pre-printed standardized Will forms which may just be filled out to make one's Will. We do not generally recommend a wholesale use of standard forms for most people, however. They frequently have the effect of putting everyone in a "straight jacket" with little room to tailor individual needs or intentions to individual situations.

However, if your situation is pretty ordinary, requiring a very simple Will, you may want to use one of these standard forms, instead. You'll just need to fill in the necessary details accordingly. A good blank standard form may, atimes, be available from a local commercial or legal stationary store. As a practical matter, however, most may not have a suitable one even for the standard needs, and it may be hard to get a "complete" will package of forms. And, even more important for you as a pro se Will-maker, most standard forms that a commercial stationer might carry are almost always drafted and designed with the attorney in mind and rarely are they particularly tailored or simplified with a pro se preparer in mind as the end user.

For your added convenience, therefore, **Do-It-Yourself Legal Publishers** makes available to its readership a specially-prepared package of forms usable by most for the standard needs. [See a sample of the Publisher's standard will form for a married person on pp. 42-3]. *To order the Publisher's standard will forms package,* just complete the **Order Form** on p. 124 giving your marital and other details and send it away to the Publisher's Legal Forms Division.

NOW, LET'S GET ON WITH THE DRAFTING OF THE WILL.

C. NUMBERED INSTRUCTIONS FOR FILLING OUT THE WILL PRACTICE WORKSHEETS [from pp. 32-35]

For Paragraph #I: Identification Clause
① Fill in your full legal names (Do not use nicknames).
② Fill in your full home address, including the town, county and state.
③ If you use or are commonly known by any other names, enter them here.

For Paragraph #II: Marital Status Clause
Pick one of these, as applicable to you:
④ If you are not married and have no children by birth or adoption, then check off (✔) this clause and be sure to transfer it (later) to the final draft copy of the Will.
⑤ If you are not married but have children, by birth or adoption, check off (✔) this clause and be sure to transfer it (later) to the final copy of the Will.
⑥ If you were previously married but divorced, then check off (✔) this clause and be sure to transfer it (later) to the final copy of the Will.
⑦ If you are currently married (or married but separated), check off (✔) this clause, upon filling in the relevant information required, and be sure to transfer it (later) to the final copy of the Will.

For Paragraph #III: Identify Whereabouts Of Children
⑧ If you have any children anywhere any time, by birth or by adoption, then check off (✔) Paragraph #III for transfer (later) to the final copy of the Will. Fill in the number of child(ren) you have, by birth and by adoption, if applicable.
⑨ Fill in, one by one, for <u>each</u> and <u>every</u> child, the full name, date of birth and current address or place of abode.

For Paragraph #IV: Payment of Estate Debts
Check off (✔) this paragraph, and transfer it (later) to the final copy of the Will.

For Paragraph #V: Burial Instructions
a. If you desire to be buried in any particular place, then fill in this subparagraph, giving the location desired in the space marked ⑩. (Such as: IN THE FAMILY BURIAL PLOT AT (address?). If, however, it doesn't matter to you where you get buried, it is not required that you provide for it in your Will.
b. If indeed, you desire that your body be cremated, then check off (✔) this subparagraph instead, and transfer it (later) to the final copy of the Will.

For Paragraph VI: Debts Forgiven, if Any
⑪ Fill in, if applicable, the names, relationship and addresses of the person or persons whose indebtedness to you you wish to forgive, if any. [If more than one person, then list each person, one by one, along with the kind and amount of indebtedness forgiven]
⑫ Enter here the amount and nature of the debt forgiven.

For Paragraph #VII: Primary Gifts & Beneficiaries
⑬ Fill in here the names, relationship or proper identification and the addresses of the persons or entities (individuals, organizations, charities, etc.) you wish to give part (or all) of your property. (Such as: My son: JOHN DOE OF 12 FIFTH AVENUE, BRONX, NY., or my children, JOHN DOE AND AGNES DOE OF 12 FIFTH AVENUE, BRONX, NY.)
⑭ Give adequate identification of the property or asset intended in this instance. (Such as: MY HOUSE AT 100 HILL ST., BRONX, BY, AND ALL THE FURNITURES AND HOUSEHOLD ITEMS IN MY APARTMENT THEREIN; or MY 1990 CADILLAC.)

For Paragraph #VIII: Gifts Continued
⑮ Fill in the names, relationship, or proper identification and addresses of the persons (individuals, organizations, etc.) you wish to give yet another portion of your property. (Such as: My daugther, JANE DOE OF 1 JOHN STREET, MANHATTAN, NY, or the CHURCH OF JESUS CHRIST AT 121 CHURCH STREET, BRONX, NY.)
⑯ Give an adequate description of the property intended. (Such as: ALL THE 200 SHARES OF XEROX COMMON STOCK I OWN; or THE PROCEEDS OF MY SAVINGS ACCOUNT WITH THE CHASE MANHATTAN BANK, PASSBOOK NO. ??).

For Paragraph #IX: Gifts Continued
⑰ Fill in, as the Numbered Instruction ⑬ or ⑮ above, for the next person(s) or organizations you wish to give something.
⑱ Give adequate identification of property or asset intended for these particular person(s) or organizations. Specify the money amount in figures as well as in words, if cash is the object of the gift. (Such as: $1,000—ONE THOUSAND DOLLARS).

For Paragraph #X: Gift/Beneficiaries of the "Residuary" Estate Left Over
⑲ Fill in the names, relationship or proper identification and the addresses of the person or persons (organizations, etc.) to whom you wish the "residuary estate" to go.[2] (The residuary estate is the remainder of your property AFTER all the debts, expenses, and everything else you already gave away are taken out.) (Such as: TO MY LAWFUL WIFE JANET DOE OF 12 BENEFIT ST., MANHATTAN, NY.; or TO MY WIFE JANET DOE OF 12 BENEFIT ST., MANHATTAN, N.Y., AND THESE MY THREE CHILDREN, DAVID, LUCY AND MICHAEL.)

---

[2]NOTE: As a matter of general practice, the "residuary estate" is usually assigned to the spouse of the testator—after every other beneficiary in the Will shall have been provided for. There is no legal rule that says, however, that it must necessarily be done that way. Be absolutely certain, though (actually, make the physical calculations to be sure), that something reasonable—the value you anticipate—will still be left over in your "residuary estate" after everything else you provided for in the Will shall have been taken out! That is *MOST, MOST IMPORTANT!*

㉑ Give the names and proper identification of the SECOND party you would wish to give the residuary estate, if the FIRST party didn't live long enough to get it.

㉑ Is there any special thing you would want this SECOND party to do with the gift, if he were to get it? If so, specify that here. (Such as: THE CARE AND EDUCATION OF MY CHILDREN, DAVID, LUCY AND MICHAEL, etc.)

㉒ Give the names and proper identification of the THIRD party you would wish to give the residuary estate, if the FIRST and SECOND parties didn't live long enough to get it.

㉓ Fill in—same as in the Numbered Instruction ㉑ above.

For Paragraph #XI: Life Insurance Proceeds

㉔ If you have a life insurance policy, fill in the policy number here.

㉕ Enter the name of the insurance company with which you are insured.

㉖ Specify any particular thing you wish the proceeds to be used for, if any, or to whom you wish the proceeds to go. (Such as: GIVEN TO MY FRIEND/BROTHER/WIFE, etc. named ??; or TO BECOME PART OF MY RESIDUARY ESTATE; or TO BE PUT IN TRUST FOR THE EDUCATION OF THESE MY CHILDREN, NAMED ??.)

For Paragraph #XII: Abatement of Gifts

㉗ Specify here the paragraph(s) to which this applies in you own true, final copy of the Will. [In the manual's sample, the relevant paragraphs would be the following: #'s VII, VIII, IX and possibly XI. Note that the "residuary estate" clause (Paragraph #X) is excluded. Generally, though, the bequests covered by this are mostly those gifts involving cash items.]

NOTE: The provision made in this paragraph is to guard against the possibility that your estate may not have enough assets to cover all the gifts you made in your Will. If that should happen (it's only a possibility!), you would probably want every other beneficiary to take less, so that your spouse and children [persons provided for in this specific example in Paragraph #X,. for example] may not be deprived.

㉘ Specify the maximum percentage (%) of the total value of your estate which you'll want your total gifts to persons other than your spouse or children not to exceed (e.g., 20% of your total estate's value? or what?).

㉙ Enter the same percentage as in the Numbered Instruction ㉘ above.

For Paragraph #XIII: Disinheriting An Heir, if Any

㉚ If you wish not to give anything to any of your children, then specify the names of such children here. (This way, you eliminate any doubts whatsoever that you may have mistakenly "overlooked" or left them out.)

For Paragraph #XIV: Possibility of Common Death by Spouses

㉛ This clause is meant to provide for the eventuality of your property having to pass through different estates in rapid succession, thereby resulting in unnecessary expenses and legal troubles to your estate. To guard against the possibility, fill in the names and proper identification of the relevant beneficiaries in this space.

㉜ Is there any special thing you would want the inheritance share which would have gone to these beneficiaries to be used for, instead? Specify that here. (Such as: BE CONSIDERED CANCELLED, AND SHALL REVERT BACK TO MY ESTATE; or GO TO THE CHILD(REN) OF THAT PARTICULAR BENEFICIARY, AND IF HE OR SHE HAS NO CHILD(REN), THEN THE GIFT SHALL BE CONSIDERED CANCELLED AND SHALL REVERT BACK TO MY ESTATE.)

For Paragraph #XV: Children's Trust Clause

㉝ If you are setting up a TRUST[3] under your Will, whereby you wish to direct your executor to set aside, say, the net proceeds of your estate for a trust whose income and principal could be used in accordance with the

---

[3]For more on trusts, see Appendix D, section B. Note that this is one of the two principal types of trusts—the so called "testamentary" trust, meaning one established under the provisions of a Will. The other type of trust is the "inter vivos" or "Living Trust"—which is a trust separately established by the individual and functional during the person's lifetime. What is relevant for you to note here, is that if your prime concern is to avoid probate, the testamentary (i.e., will-established) trust does not accomplish that. Only a living trust does. With a testamentary trust, on the other hand, the trust can come into being only if and after your Will shall have cleared the probate court and the executor has been discharged. Thus, in effect, the testamentary trust is just as subject to all of the delay, expense, and publicity which ordinarily go with the probate process!

instructions in your Will, then enter here the name of the person you appoint as the Trustee, the one who is to manage that trust.

㉞ Give the address of the said trustee.

㉟ Give the names and proper identification of the NEXT person or institution you wish to appoint, if the first trustee should die or be unable to complete the job.

㊱ Give the address of this SECOND trustee.

㊲ Give the names and proper identification of the THIRD person or institution you wish to appoint, if the first and second trustees you designated should die or be unable to complete the job.

㊳ Give the address of this THIRD trustee.

㊴ Give the name and address of the final person or institution you wish to appoint to act as trustee, in the event that none of the previous three is able to complete the job for any reason.

> **NOTE**: As a matter of general practice, the final party designated as trustee is usually a trust bank or other financial institution mainly because, unlike human beings who can come and go, institutions would usually always be there. But you don't necessarily have to appoint an institution. Besides, their service fees are often sizable. Note, also, that you don't necessarily have to appoint more than one or two trustees, but it's good practice to do so. Your designated "guardian" (your spouse, adult children, trusted friend or relative, etc.) could be one and the same person as the person you choose to serve as trustee. And the Executor of the Will could also be one and the same person as the designated trustee. You just have to make the decisions as you best see fit or prefer!

For Paragraph #XVI:

㊵ Enter the age or time at which you want the entitlements of your minor children (or others) to be handed over to them—if you want it held in trust for them until they reach a certain age. Give the time or age, such as: 21, 25, or ??.

㊶ Enter the appropriate age (or time) same as in Instruction #㊵ above.

㊷ Enter the appropriate age (or time) same as in Instruction #㊵ above.

For Paragraph #XVII:

If paragraphs #XV and #XVI above are applicable to you, then check off (✔) this paragraph and transfer it (later) to the final, true copy of the Will.

For Paragraph #XVIII: (Trustee's Powers & Duties)

If paragraphs #'s XV, XVI, and XVII above are applicable to you, then check off (✔) this paragraph and transfer it (later) to the final copy of the Will.

For Paragraph #XIX: Funding of Estate Taxes, if Applicable

a. If your estate is subject to some death or estate taxes (or other kind of taxes), how and what do you want them to be paid out of? If you want them to be borne entirely by your residuary estate, then check off this sub-paragraph and transfer it (later) to the final, true copy of the Will.

b. If, on the other hand, you want such taxes to be shared equally (or in any other referred proportion) among some or all of the beneficiaries named in the Will, then check off this sub-paragraph and transfer it (or a variation thereof) to the final, true copy of the Will.

For Paragraph #XX: Disposition of Business, if Applicable

㊸ If you have a family business, investment, etc., which you wish to be continued (or to be liquidated), fill in its name and location here.

㊹ State how you wish that business or investment to be disposed of. (Such as: CONTINUED UNTIL MY ELDEST SON SHALL REACH THE AGE OF 21 A WHICH POINT MY SAID SON SHALL DECIDE; or SOLD AND LIQUIDATED AND THE PROCEEDS USED FOR_____??_____.

㊺ Fill in the names and addresses of the person or persons you appoint to manage the business or investment, if applicable.

For Paragraph #XXI: Naming a Guardian for the children, if Applicable

㊻ Give the names, relationship and proper identification of the SECOND person you would want to act as the guardian of any minor children you have, if your spouse should die or be unable to do the job for any reason.

NOTE: Where there are minor children or beneficiaries who are not competent to manage investments or their inheritance, both a guardian and a trustee could be designated. A guardianship would usually take effect after (and in the event that) the second parent dies, and terminate when the minor reaches the age of maturity; a trust my be in operation consecutively—that is, during the lives of the surviving spouse, the minors, and perhaps the grand-children. Often, the guardian's duty is limited to that of looking after "the person" of the minor, as differentiated from looking after his "property." A guardian can administer the inheritance of a minor. However, it should be noted that in regard to a minor, having a trust has many advantages over a guardianship. A guardianship is generally a much more expensive method of administering the minor's property in that the guardian's powers of investment are more limited, and so are his freedom to act on the minor's behalf (requirements to post bond, give annual accountings, and to get the court's consent to use the minor's assets for the benefit of the minor, etc.). A trustee, on the other hand, can be given broad discretionary powers and can act with little or no restrictions in investment matters.

㊼ Enter the address of the intended SECOND guardian.

㊽ List the names and ages of the specific minor child or children who should be covered by this guardianship.

㊾ Give the age at which you want the guardianship for the children to end.

㊿ Give the names and proper identification of the THIRD person you would want to act as the guardian, in the event that none of the previous guardians is able to do the job for any reason.

(51) Enter the address of the intended THIRD guardian.

For Paragraph #XXII: Designation of the Executor

(52) Fill in the names and proper identification and address of the person (or persons) you wish to appoint as the EXECUTOR (or EXECUTRIX, if a female) of your Will. (Such as: MY WIFE, JANET DOE, OF 12 BENEFIT ST., MANHATTAN, NY.; or MY BUSINESS PARTNER, EDWARD MARTIN, OF 2 BUSINESS ST., MAPLE, NJ.)

NOTE: The Executor or Executrix is a very important person in any Will. He or she is the person responsible for carrying out the provisions of the Will. See Appendix E of the manual (at p. 111) for more on the executor's responsibilities.

(53) Enter the names and proper identification of the SECOND person you wish to appoint as Executor, if the first executor should die or be unable to do the job for any reason.

(54) Enter the address of the intended second executor or executrix.

(55) Enter the names and proper identification of the THIRD person you wish to appoint as Executor, if the first two executors should die or be unable to do the job for any reason.

(56) Enter the address of the intended THIRD executor or executrix.

For Paragraph #XXIII: Marital Deduction

This paragraph is meant to allow the testator to preserve the opportunity of still getting the tax benefits of the "marital deduction," even if both spouses were to die in a common disaster (see Chapter 8 at p. 65). To guard against having to lose this benefit, check off this paragraph (if married) for transfer (later) to the final, true copy of the Will.

For Paragraph #XXIV: Organ Donation

If you happen to wish to make a donation of your body (or specific organs thereof) after your death for use for medical purposes, then check off (✔) this paragraph for it's transfer to the final copy of the Will.

(57) Fill in here the names of the person(s) or institutions to which you wish to make the donation (Such as: THE PHYSICIAN IN ATTENDANCE AT MY DEATH; or THE HOSPITAL IN WHICH I DIE.

(58) Fill in here the purposes you want the donated body organs or parts to be used for (Such as: ANY PURPOSE AUTHORIZED BY LAW; or MEDICAL EDUCATION; or TRANSPLANTATION; or RESEARCH.)

For Paragraph #XXV:

㊾ through ㊱. Check off paragraph #XXV for transfer to the final, true copy of the Will; provide the spaces marked ㊾, ㊿, and ㊱, for the day, month and year, respectively, on which you sign the Will.

㊲ and ㊳. Provide these spaces in the final, true copy of the Will. You sign the Will (later) in the space marked ㊲ and then print your name below the signature in ㊳.

For Paragraph #XXVI:

㊴ Check off paragraph #XXVI for transfer to the final true copy of the Will; provide the space marked ㊴ for a witness to enter the number of counted pages comprising the Will at the time of the signing ceremony.

㊵ through ㊸. Provide these spaces in the final, true copy of your Will. (Each of your witnesses will sign and enter his/her address in each of these spots at the time of the signing ceremony.)

C. YOU HAVE NOW COMPLETED MAKING UP THE DRAFT COPY OF YOUR WILL. NOW, TYPE UP AND FINISH THE WILL

Now, you've just completed making up the initial drafting of your Will—assuming you've just followed through the steps and instructions set forth in Section B above. But there are a few little things left: TYPING OUT A FINAL PERFECT COPY OF THE WILL. Now, run through the PRACTICE WORKSHEETS once again, from its first page down; and, carefully and in order, type (or print) out on separate sheets of paper the complete Will with the contents of each and every clause or paragraph that you filled in or checked off now included. Type (or print) out everything onto separate sheets of white paper to make out a final, true copy of your Will. (Number the pages of your completed Will at the top of each paper and be sure to provide at the bottom left corner of each paper, a space for you to initial the Will). You should make two (and only two) final copies of the Will; you may use carbon paper, but make sure that each copy is exactly the same in contents.)

Avoid erasing, crossing out or other corrections in your final draft to avoid any suspicions that might arise later that such changes might have been slipped in by someone other than you. (Note: if your final Will copy contains any substantial errors, always retype completely that entire page.)

Run down the contents of your final draft once again and carefully compare the items on the final draft with the items on the practice sheets. Did you get everything? Is there anything you might like to adjust or add in the final draft? Is your intent and the language of the Will—every sentence, paragraph—clear and unambiguous? Counter-check and make the necessary adjustments, accordingly. Then type (or write) out a final, perfect copy.

NEXT, COMPLETE (AND TYPE UP) ON A SEPARATE SHEET OF PAPER, THE DOCUMENT TITLED "Affidavit Of Subscribing or Attesting Witnesses" (Sample on p. 36). Attach that (the final perfect copy) to the Will; that document will come in handy in the next step, the signing and witnessing occasion.

IT'S NOW DONE. The next order of business is the execution phase—the SIGNING AND WITNESSING of the Will you've just finished drafting. For that, turn to Chapter Five at p. 37 for the procedures.

D. My Last Will And Testament

SAMPLE WILL (The Practice Worksheets)
(See the Numbered Instructions for completing this Will form on pp. 26-31)

Last Will And Testament Of_____ [Enter the Will maker's legal name in full]

I.   I, Mr/Mrs_____**①**_____ , a married/unmarried* person, residing at_____**②**_____, also known by the name(s) of_____**③**_____ do hereby revoke all former Wills and codicils made by me.

II. **④** I have never been married and have no children, by birth or adoption; OR:
  ⑤ I have never been married, but I have _____ child(ren), as fully detailed in Paragraph _____ below; OR:
  ⑥ I was previously married to Mr/Mrs_____ *(previous spouse's name in full)*, which marriage was terminated on or about this date _____19_____ , by divorce/death*; OR:
  ⑦ I am currently married to_____*(his/her name in full)*, and have been so married since _____19_____ [Or, if applicable: I have been married to Mr/Mrs_____ since _____19_____, but have been separated and living apart from him/her since _____19___]

III.   I have _____**⑧**_____ child(ren) who are living; and their names, dates (or appropriate dates) of birth and addresses are _____**⑨**_____ .

IV.   I direct that all my lawful debts, including funeral expenses, expenses for my last illness, if applicable, and the expense of the administration of my estate, be paid by my Executor or Executrix named below, or the successor thereof, as soon as practicable after my death.

Va.   I direct that I be buried in _____**⑩**_____ .
Vb.   I direct that my body be cremated after my death.

VI.   I hereby release and forgive the following person/persons_____**⑪**_____ of his/her (their) indebtedness to me in the sum of $_____**⑫**_____ .

VII.   I give to_____**⑬**_____ these assets/property described as follows:** _____**⑭**_____ _____ .

VIII.   I give to _____**⑮**_____ these assets/property described as follows:_____ _____**⑯**_____ .

IX.   I give to _____**⑰**_____ the sum of _____**⑱**_____ .

X.   I give all the rest and residue of my estate (hereinafter to be called my "residuary estate"), of whatever nature and wherever located, to _____**⑲**_____ . In the event he/she (they) dies before me, or within 60 days after my death, then I hereby direct that my residuary estate be given
Testator's Initials:_____
Date:_____

---

*Cross out one or the other, as necessary.

**NOTE: If any of the property you are giving away is "encumbered" (property on which some money is owed, such as mortgaged real estate or personal property with a lien or chattel mortgage), you may wish to give the property free of such liability, and to have the encumbrance paid out of your estate funds. To accomplish this, just add a phrase to that effect, such as: "This gift is to be given to this beneficiary, free and clear of any debts owed by me on it." But note that if (whenever) you make such a provision, you should be sure that your entire estate has enough value and money in it to allow for this, and/or that your "residuary estate" (Paragraph X of the Will) will have sufficient money in it to make room for and allow for this.

to _____ **(20)** _____ and further direct that it be used as follows:_____
_____ **(21)** _____ . And in the event that none of the beneficiaries named in this paragraph immediately survives me, then I direct that my residuary estate shall be given to _____ **(22)** _____ , and further direct that it be used as follows: _____ **(23)** _____ .

XI. I direct that the proceeds of my life insurance policy, Policy No. _____ **(24)** _____, kept with the _____ **(25)** _____ Insurance Company, shall be used as follows: _____ _____ **(26)** _____

XII. Notwithstanding anything contained in this Will to the contrary, if the total gifts made under paragraphs _____ **(27)** _____ of this Will shall exceed _____ **(28)** _____ percent of the gross value of my estate, I hereby direct that in that event all such gifts in the said paragraphs shall be abated and reduced proportionately, so that all of those gifts added together shall not exceed _____ **(29)** _____ percent of the gross value of my estate.

XIII. I expressly want it known that the following of my child(ren) who have not been bequeathed anything in this Will, namely: _____ **(30)** _____, are not mistakenly overlooked, but are deliberately left nothing because I do not wish to leave them anything.* No such person or persons shall therefore object, directly or indirectly, to the provisions of this Will, or in any way challenge or otherwise contest the contents and provisions thereof.

XIV. With respect to the following beneficiaries named in this Will, namely:_____ _____ **(31)** _____ , if any of them and I should die at the same time (in a common accident or disaster, or from any other causes), or if any of them should die before me or within 60 days of my death, I direct that unless provided for otherwise elsewhere in this Will, the gifts made herein to the said beneficiaries shall _____ **(32)** _____ .

XV. I appoint Mr./Mrs. _____ **(33)** _____ of _____ **(34)** _____ as Trustee under this Will, to act without bond and full powers. If the first named Trustee shall be either unavailable or unwilling or unable to serve for any reason, I name and appoint Mr./Mrs. _____ **(35)** _____ of _____ **(36)** _____ as Trustee under the same powers and conditions. And if the named second Trustee shall be either unavailable or unwilling or unable to serve for any reason, I name and appoint Mr./Mrs._____ **(37)** _____ of _____ **(38)** _____ as Trustee under the same powers and conditions. If none of the above parties is available or able to act, then I appoint_____ _____ **(39)** _____ as Trustee.

XVI. If any beneficiary under this Will shall be under the age of _____ **(40)** _____ at the time he or she becomes entitled to the distribution herein, then the payment of such entitlement shall not be made, but shall be deferred until such beneficiary reaches the age of _____ **(41)** _____ . Such entitlement shall, instead, be held by the Trustee herein appointed under this Will, in trust for and on behalf of that beneficiary. The Trustee is hereby directed to invest the said entitlement in such income yielding ventures as the Trustee may deem proper, and the income as well as such amounts of the principal as are necessary, even to the extent of all, shall be applied to the support, general welfare and education of the said beneficiary until he or she reaches the age of_____ _____ **(42)** _____ whereupon the remaining principal and income of the trust, if any, shall be paid to the beneficiary.

Testator's Initials:_____
Date:_____
_____

*__NOTE__: In instances where the testator has no spouse or children, a similar clause would, instead, be used to name the testator's parents, brothers and sisters, if he wishes to disinherit these relatives without leaving the Will open to possible contest, since such relatives (i.e., parents, brothers and sisters) would be next in line to inherit from him in the absence of a spouse or children.

XVII. If any beneficiary for whom an entitlement is held in trust under this Will should die before having received his or her trust share, then when he or she dies, the remaining share shall be paid to his or her living child(ren) in equal proportions per child; and if he or she has no child(ren), then it shall be paid to my then living issues.

XVIII. I grant my Trustees the full powers and discretion to invest, buy or sell, hire professional help, and otherwise manage and administer the trust assets based on such conditions as the Trustees may in their sole discretion deem proper and necessary, all without bond or court order, and always keeping in mind the best interest and welfare of the trust beneficiaries.

XIXa. I direct that transfer, estate, inheritance, and other such taxes or interests assessed on my gross taxable estate, if any, shall NOT be apportioned, but shall be paid out of my residuary estate. [See paragraph 4 of this sample Will].

XIXb. I direct that transfer, estate, inheritance, and other such taxes or interests assessed on my gross taxable estate, if any, shall be apportioned proportionately by the executor herein according to the value of the bequests received, as assessed by the executor, and be paid in such proportions by the beneficiaries named in this Will. [See paragraph IV of this sample Will.]

XX. I direct that my business/investments/securities* named and located as follows:_____
_____ (43) _____ shall be ____ (44) ____ after my death, and shall be under the control and management of _____ (45) _____ .

XXI. If my spouse shall not survive me or is incapacitated, and it is necessary that a guardian be appointed for our child(ren), I name and appoint Mr./Mrs._____ (46) _____
of this address _____ (47) _____ to be the guardian of the following of my children, each named and aged _____ (48) _____ until each has reached the age of ____ (49) ____ . If the FIRST guardian shall cease or be unable to serve for any reason, I name and appoint Mr./Mrs._____ (50) _____
of the address _____ (51) _____ as their Guardian until they attain their majority ages. No bond shall be required of any guardian appointed by this Will.

XXII. I appoint and nominate Mr./Mrs._____ (52) _____
of this address _____ (52) _____ as Executor (or Executrix) of this Will, to serve without bond, and I hereby grant full powers and authority to the said Executor to use the fullest discretion in all matters and questions relevant to the carrying out of the matters directed in this Will, all without bond or court order. The said powers, authority and discretion shall include (but shall not be limited to) complete authority to sell at public or private sale, for cash or credit, with or without security, and/or to invest, reinvest, mortgage, compromise and settle claims, lease, pledge and dispose of all property, at such times and upon such terms and conditions as he/she may solely determine, all without bond or court order. If the above-named FIRST Executor (or Executrix) shall die before me or shall cease or be unable to serve for any reason, then I appoint and nominate Mr./Mrs._____ (53) _____ of this address_____
_____ (54) _____ to serve in the same capacity and under the same powers and conditions as described above. And if the SECOND Execuor (or executrix) shall die before me or shall cease or be unable to serve for any reason, then I appoint and nominate Mr./Mrs. _____ (55) _____
of this address _____ (56) _____ to serve in the same capacity and under the same powers and conditions as described above.

Testator's Initials:_____
Date:_____

_____

*Cross out the unnecessary one or ones, as applicable.

XXIII. In the event that my wife/husband* and I shall die together as a result of a common disaster, or under circumstances such that it cannot be readily determines who dies before the other, it shall be presumed for the purposes of this Will and my estate that I died before her/him.

XXIV. I hereby make an anatomical donation, hereinafter described, to take effect upon my death. I donate my body or any needed organs or parts,** to the following persons, medical institutions or storage banks _____(57)_____ for use for the following purposes _____ _____(58)_____ And I direct my Executor to carry out the said donation.

XXV. IN WITNESS WHEREOF, I hereby sign, seal, and declare this as my Last Will and Testament on this date, the ___(59)___ day of the month of ____(60)____ 19 __(61)__

Signed: X _____(62)_____
(Will-maker's signature in full)

Name of Will-maker (print): _____(63)_____

Attestation of Witnesses

XXVI. Each of us, the undersigned witnesses, hereby declare under the penalty of perjury, that on the date above set forth, the foregoing document, consisting of ___(64)___ pages, including this page, was signed and sealed by the above named person as the Testator or Will-maker, and that at the time of that signature, the said person stated that the document he/she*** signed was his/her*** LAST WILL AND TESTAMENT; we declare that at the time when the said person signed the document, he/she*** appeared to be of sound mind and memory and under no duress or constraint. Whereupon, at the said testator's request and in the testator's presence and in the presence of each other, we hereby sign our names below as witnesses thereto:

SIGNATURE: X _____(65)_____ NAME (print): _____

residing at _____
(enter person's full home address)

SIGNATURE: X _____(66)_____ NAME (print): _____

residing at _____
(enter person's full home address)

SIGNATURE: X _____(67)_____ NAME (print): _____

residing at _____
(enter person's full home address)

---

*Cross out one party, as applicable. Remember that for marital deduction purposes, the spouse who owns the smaller estate ought to be the one who is to be presumed to survive the other. The tax code requires that, in order to get the marital deduction allowance, there must be one spouse who survives the other. What this means, simply, is that if a couple should die, say in a common disaster so that it is not clear which spouse died last, then the marital deduction allowance would be lost to both spouses and to the estate—since neither one survived the other. Hence, to get around this eventuality, you simply provide a clause in the Will which merely states that in the event of a common death it should be "presumed" that a designated spouse—usually the one who owns the smaller estate (say the wife)—is the survivor. This way, in the event of death in a common disaster, the bulk of the estate assets will pass to her, but the marital deduction allowance available to the larger estate will even out her estate for tax purposes. (Note that this device can only work where one spouse owns a far larger estate than the other. The clause provision in the Will is required <u>only</u> in the Will of the one with the larger estate.)

**Or, if you prefer, you can specify particular organs or parts of the body that are to be taken, as follows: "I donate the following organs or parts of my body (specify them)."

***Cross out one, as applicable.

36

Copyright © 1994, Do-It-Yourself Legal Publishers, Newark, NJ 07012

(Addendum to the Last Will and Testament)

Affidavit of Subscribing or Attesting Witnesses TO THE WILL

THE WILL OF MR/MRS/MS: _____ *(Testator enters his/her full name here)* _____, Testator.

STATE OF_____)
COUNTY OF_____) ss.: ← *(Notary Public to complete these)*

ON THIS DATE, the _____ day of _____ 19____, personally appeared before me, a Notary Public duly authorized to administer oath in and for the above captioned County and State, the undersigned persons, who are known to me or to me made known.

WHEREUPON, the said persons, as each of them individually signed and appended his/her respective name and address to this document, and while being severally sworn, individually and collectively stated under oath, that they witnessed the execution of the WILL of Mr/Mrs/Ms: *(full name of the will-maker is entered here)* , the within named Testator(trix), on_____ *(date when the will was signed)* _____ 19_____; that the Testator(trix), in their presence, subscribed to and signed the Will at the end, and, that at the time of the said making of the subscription, he/she declared the instrument to be the Testator(trix)'s Last Will and Testament; that at the request of the Testator(trix) and in the Testator(trix)'s sight and presence, and in the sight and presence of each other, the said persons witnessed the execution of the Will by the Testator(trix) by subcribing their own names as witnesses to it; and that he Testator(trix) at the time of the execution of the Will, appeared to them to be of full age and sound mind and memory and was in all respects competent to make a will and was not under any restraint.

THE SUBSCRIBING WITNESSES FURTHER STATE under oath that this Afifdavit is hereby being executed at the request of Mr/Mrs/Ms._____ *(full name of the Will maker)* _____, the Testator(trix) who made the Will; and that at the time of the execution of this Affidavit, the original Will, above described, was exhibited to them and they identified it as such a Will by their signatures appearing on it as subscribing witnesses.

SIGNATURES, NAMES & ADDRESSES OF WITNESSES:

1. Signature ✗:*(1st witness signs here—in the Notary Public's presence)*
Print Name: *(by 1st witness)*_____
Address: *(of 1st witness)*_____

Severally subscribed and sworn to before me on _____
_____19____

2. Signature ✗:*(2nd witness signs here—in the Notary Public's presence)*
Print Name: *(by 2nd witness)*_____
Address: *(of 2nd witness)*_____

....
(Notary Public)

3. Signature ✗:*(3rd witness signs here—in the Notary Public's presence)*
Print Name: *(by 3rd witness)*_____
Address: *(of 3rd witness)*_____

Chapter 5
LET'S SIGN THE WILL: THE PROCEDURES FOR THE ALL-IMPORTANT "EXECUTION" OF THE WILL

After a Will is drawn up (the subject matter of the preceding Chapter 4), the next order of business is the **"execution"** (the signing) of the Will. To sum it up IN ONE WORD, SUFFICE IT SIMPLY TO SAY THIS: THE SIGNING OF THE WILL IS THE KEY ITEM, EASILY THE SINGLE MOST VITAL EVENT IN THE MAKING OF A VALID WILL. *Therefore, this is an extremely important and most serious business and should be treated with the utmost care and attention to every detail by the Will-maker.*

A. SOME RECOMMENDED PRACTICAL "CEREMONIES" FOR A VALID SIGNING

The relevant laws of each state stipulate certain basic procedures or requirements for a valid "execution" (signing) of the Will. ***It's to ensure that the requirements of every state are met, whichever state it may be, that we suggest this: you must strictly follow these step-by-step "ceremonies" or procedures to sign your Will.***

THESE ARE:

FIRST: The first thing you should do, is to look up the basic requirements for the signing and witnessing of a Will under the rules of your state — how many witnesses are required, and of what minimum age, whether the beneficiaries in the Will could also be used as witnesses, whether your state requires the Will to be notarized, and the like. (These requirements are fully listed in Appendix A at p. 75.)

SECOND: Thereafter, set a date for the signing event, and assemble your witnesses accordingly. [It's also advis able to have the persons who are to serve as your executors, guardians, trustees, appear at the Will-signing event, if practical, though this is not a legal requirement, unless of course, such persons are also to serve as witnesses.]

NOTE: Of course, most states require just two witnesses, and a fewer number of states (Louisiana, Maine, New Hampshire, Puerto Rico, South Carolina and Vermont), require three. But remember this: *it is still very much advisable, whenever possible, to have __more__ witnesses than the law of a given state specifically requires.* This way, if one of the witnesses you used should later die or leave the state or be unavailable for any reason, your Will would still have sufficient number of witnesses on it. Furthermore, even if your state's laws would permit otherwise, you should still try to get as your witnesses, persons who are not named as executors, guardians, trustees or beneficiaries under your Will. Also, it would be better to look for people with no unusual records of criminality, fraud, dishonesty, mental illness, or even some conditions of physical impairment (deafness, dumbness, blindness, and the like.) And finally, it is always preferable, whenever possible, to select as witnesses persons who are in good health and much younger than you. The prime reason why it is generally preferable to pick "credible" and younger persons is this: the Will would have to be "probated" — presented to a court for proof of it's genuineness — someday. And, of course, it is on these witnesses that the court and your executor will primarily rely for this proof.

THIRD: O.K. Let's assume that you've now assembled your (credible) witnesses on the appointed execution date. [All witnesses must be present at the same time.] And, in front of you, is a copy of your Will — the final, true draft. Admit nobody else, except you and your witnesses into the room. Now, briefly inform the witnesses that the document you have in front of you, about to sign, is your Last Will and Testament. (You may say something like: *"Gentlemen, this paper is my Last Will and Testament. I have read it, and with sound mind and without pressure and without any undue influence from anyone, I ask you to witness my signature, and to sign your names after me as witnesses."*)

And with that statement, as the witnesses watch you, you initial and date each and every page of the Will (just <u>one</u> original copy) at the bottom left margin, and then sign your name (in full) on the last page. SIGN IN COLORED INK ONLY. (This way, the original document could be differentiated.) Then, print your name just below your signature. Fill in the date of the signing at the last page. (Sign only ONE original copy, but retain an unsigned copy.)

FOURTH: It will now be the turn of the witnesses to sign. Ask each of the witnesses to read the paragraph on the last page of the Will under the caption ***"Attestation Of Witnesses"*** — the one just below your own signature which begins with "Each of us, the undersigned witnesses ..." (Note that it is not necessary that the contents of the Will be read by or made known to the witnesses; in fact, it is advised against!)

Then, as you watch each of the witnesses, they would take turns to sign and enter their individual addresses in the spaces provided for that. Only after that — after all of the witnesses have signed their own names — should anybody in the group leave the room, or be joined by anyone else not in the signing group.

NOTE: The central point of engaging in the formalities ("ceremonies") of Will-signing should be clearly borne in mind. The idea is to make the event MEMORABLE to those who participated, especially to the witnesses — to make the event "stick out" in their minds, so that they'll always recall the event, however remotely or vaguely, if or when it should ever become necessary that they be called upon to do so.

FIFTH: **HAVE THE WITNESSES NOTARIZE A FORM, IF POSSIBLE.** There's one more thing before you're done: your witnesses should sign and ***notarize*** the one-page paper you have prepared—the self-proving *AFFIDAVIT OF SUBSCRIBING WITNESSES.* Here is what you do: After the signing ceremony for the Will, you should have your witnesses (all of them) stop by a Notary Public's office with the document TITLED ***"Affidavit Of Subscribing Witnesses."*** (See sample of this document on p. 36.) This could be done on the same day of the Will signing affair; or later — but not too much later. Preferable, do it all at once at the same time and date. And at the Notary Public's office (generally located in most banks, real estate and lawyer's offices, corner drug stores and the like), each witness will sign his or her name on the Affidavit and the Notary Public will "notarize" (i.e., stamp and sign) the document in turn, as proof that the witnesses did appear before him and swore to and signed the Affidavit. Thereafter, you should get the notarized Affidavit back from your witnesses. Attach this notarized Affidavit to your original Will. Put these two documents (the Will and the Affidavit) in a thick envelope and seal it with extra glue. Write the words "LAST WILL AND TESTAMENT OF (YOUR NAME)" on the envelope.

NOTE: Failure to make or to have this Self-Proving Affidavit does not make a Will that is otherwise properly drafted and executed invalid. The Will will still remain valid quite alright. Having the Affidavit, though, serves a great practical use and value, and should, whenever practical, be obtained by the testator, unless it's not remotely possible for some reason. Here's it's central advantage: when such an affidavit is signed and available, the probate court will, when it comes time to probate the Will, simply accept ("admit") the affidavit as sufficient "proof" of the genuineness of the Will, and the witnesses would not have to be required to appear in court and give oral testimony to prove the Will. This, obviously, is a tremendous advantage in terms of the time, money and effort it would take in "admitting a Will to probate."

NOW IT IS FINALLY DONE AND YOU HAVE A VALID WILL!!!

B. SOME FINAL ISSUES, INCLUDING FUTURE UPDATING AND AMENDMENT OF THE WILL

It is done, of course. And you may now rest, assured that you at least have a valid Will. But while you do that, it would help to keep a few final facts in mind. They are:

1. WHERE TO PUT AWAY THE WILL DOCUMENT

And what do you do with the Will, where do you keep it? Keep the sealed envelope containing the Will in a safe, accessible place. There is no rule about where a Will should particularly be kept, but the general rule is to keep a Will where it can be readily reached by the testator's spouse and/or executor/executrix. A safe deposit box is often (but not always) preferred;[1] and you may also keep it with a professional organization. Some estate planners advise against keeping your Will (the original) in your home on the ground that it can be easily destroyed by fire. Wherever you keep the Will, just be sure that your spouse, trusted friend or relative, or the executor, knows about it, and that they could have easy access to it in an emergency situation. Some banks may also keep your Will for you in their capacity as an executor or trustee.

Keep the unsigned copy of the Will at a different place (at home or in some other convenient place) in case you need to refresh your memory on details of the Will from time to time.

2. AMENDMENT OR REVOCATION OF THE WILL

If, in the future, you wish to amend or change some aspects of your Will, or to cancel ("revoke") it altogether, what do you do? It's simple. To amend, change, add to, or take out any aspects of a Will, all you have to do is execute a document known as a CODICIL. (See sample of this document at p. 40 of the manual.) To execute such a codicil, however, you have to follow the same formalities and conditions outlined in Section A above for the signing of a Will. (Note: Don't ever try to "slip" in changes in the text of the Will; you could throw the entire Will into question that way.)

To revoke a Will, all you have to do is either destroy completely that existing Will, or make a new Will, while making sure, though, that the new Will contains a statement specifically saying that you revoke all and any previous Wills and Codicils you made before. Something like: "I hereby revoke all Wills and codicils previously made by me."

3. MAINTAIN A MEMO & ITEMIZED LIST OF DATA AND INSTRUCTIONS TO INFORM AND AID YOUR EXECUTOR

True, no state or jurisdiction statutorily requires that a Will-maker should specifically list or itemize all his possessions in a Will (in deed nobody really does or should do that). Nevertheless, it would be advisable for a testator to make up a separate MEMORANDUM listing the details and particulars of his most essential possessions (his bank accounts, cars, names of companies carrying his life insurance, real estate holdings, names of stocks and bonds owned and with whom kept, pension and profit-sharing benefits, debts or receivables outstanding, etc), and even more importantly, giving the essential details and instructions on their particular locations, how he/she wants certain items of special or sentimental value to him or to the family to be distributed, where or how to locate help in settling the estate, and so on and so forth. ***Attach a copy of this memorandum to your original Will at all times*** and attempt to update it from time to time. This way, in an emergency situation, your property can easily be located without the possibility that some might be missed, and some other helpful details of more personal or immediate nature will be at the executor's disposal. [For a good illustrative sample of such a memo, see the listing in Appendix B on pp. 79-84, titled "Letter Of Instructions & Information To Aid In Distribution & Settlement Of The Estate And Affairs Of Fala Merced Colo, a/k/a Merced Colo."]

4. PERIODICALLY REVIEW & UPDATE YOUR WILL

It's strongly advised that you make it a habit to review your Will periodically (say, every few years), especially if you are the kind of person in whose life many rapid changes occur—birth of a new child or grandchild, acquisition or sale of new assets, marriage or remarriage, divorce, etc. This way, you'll make sure that your Will remains ever current and leaves no room for possible legal challenges or misunderstandings.

To amend or modify your Will, you may use the CODICIL method (see Form on p. 40) to do so. However, be reminded that this method of amending or changing the provisions of a Will is generally advisable only when

---

[1]In certain states, e.g., Ohio, the local Probate or Surrogate Court clerk's office do undertake to safe-keeping the Wills of Individuals for a nominal fee. One problem with keeping a Will in safe deposit boxes is that the banks often require a special court order before they'll allow access even to a surviving spouse or the executor. So, first check with your bank where you maintain your safe deposit box about its policy with respect to this before you decide to keep your papers in the box therein.

just some few minor changes are required to be made. For one thing, it would appear quite sloppy—and open to all manner of suspicious speculations and potential challenges—to make extensive or wholesale changes through a Codicil. Much more acceptable and risk-free in such a situation, would be simply to discard the old Will altogether and make a completely new Will. If a Codicil is not properly executed, it may have no effect whatsoever on the original Will; the provisions of the original will, in effect, will still stand.

CAUTION: Be warned, however, that whenever you change your Will, or change any term, provision, or even a simple word or wording, therein, whether by Codicil or drawing up a new Will, you will have to go through all the signing and witnessing formalities and ceremonies all over, exactly as outlined for a regular Will-signing (pp. 37-8), including having the witnesses sign a notarized SELF-PROVING AFFIDAVIT for the basic Will, or for the Codicil, if applicable.

Codicil To My Last Will

(Sample Form for Amendment of a Will)

I, Mr/Mrs/Miss_____, a resident of_____, do hereby make this a Codicil to my Last Will and Testament, dated the _____day of _____, 19_____.

1. I revoke paragraph_____of my said Will, and direct that the property described therein, shall now go to_____ of this address _____.

2. I hereby revoke the appointment of_____as the _____ under my said will, and appoint, instead, Mr/Mrs_____ of this address_____ to serve with the same power and authority.

   IN WITNESS WHEREOF, I hereby sign, seal and declare this as a Codicil to my Last Will and Testament, on this_____day of_____19_____.

SIGNED: ✗ _____
Testator's Signature (and full name)
Name (print)_____

ATTESTATION OF WITNESSES

The foregoing document consisting of this page, was signed, sealed and declared by the above-named party as a Codicil to his (her) last Will and Testament, dated the_____day of_____, 19___, and was so signed in our presence, and at his request and in the testator's presence, and the presence of each other, we hereby subscribe our names as witnesses thereto, and we declare that at the time when the said party signed this instrument, he appeared to be of sound mind and memory and under no duress or constraint.

SIGNATURE: ✗ _____residing at_____
Name (Print)_____

SIGNATURE: ✗ _____residing at_____
Name (Print)_____

SIGNATURE: ✗ _____residing at_____
Name (Print)_____

ONE-STOP PROCEDURE FOR EXECUTING A "SELF-PROVING" WILL BEFORE THE NOTARY PUBLIC

For a **one-stop** signing of the Will (by you) and the signing of the AFFIDAVIT OF SUBSCRIBING or ATTESTING WITNESSES (by your witnesses), you may prefer this procedure. First, assemble all your three (or two) witnesses. Then go with them to a local Notary Public, taking with you the <u>original</u> copies of your Will and the Affidavit of Subscribing (Attesting) Witnesses form. THEN HERE'S WHAT HAPPENS:

TESTATOR: You, the testator (the person making the will), and your three witnesses assemble at the Notary Public's office. You sign the will as all the witnesses watch you, and as you say out loudly the appropriate statement to this effect: *"Ladies and/or gentlemen, this is my last Will and Testament, and I am signing it voluntarily and with my full mind, and invite all of you to witness this and to sign the Will after me as witnesses."*

WITNESSES: The three witnesses, as the Notary Public and everyone watch, will then <u>individually</u> sign the papers in TWO places—one at the end of the Will, and the other on the Affidavit of Subscribing Witnesses form.

The following is then said aloud:

NOTARY [turning to you]:
"John Smith (the testator's full name), do you identify this document as your Last Will and Testament, do you wish it to be so regarded, and have you signed it of your own free will?"

TESTATOR [you]: "Yes."

NOTARY: "And have you requested these persons who are gathered here to witness your signature and to make an affidavit confirming your execution of this will?"

TESTATOR: "I have."

NOTARY [turning to the witnesses]:
"The witnesses will please raise their right hands. Do all of you individually as well as collectively, declare under oath, that Mr. Smith has identified this document as his Last Will and Testament and stated that he wishes it to be so regarded?"

WITNESSES: (in unison) "He has."

NOTARY: "Has he signed it in your presence, saying that he was doing so of his own free will?"

WITNESSES: (in unison) "He has."

NOTARY: "And did Mr. Smith at the time he signed the document appear to be of sound mind and legal age and free of any undue influence?"

WITNESSES: (in unison) "Yes."

NOTARY: "Has each of you, in his presence and at his request, and in the presence of each other, affixed your signatures to this document as witnesses, and have you made this affidavit at his request?"

WITNESSES: (in unison) "We have."

NOTARY: "You may put your hands down."

The Notary Public then affixes his notary stamp on the witnesses' affidavit (the AFFIDAVIT OF SUBSCRIBING WITNESSES) and notarizes the affidavit.

Last Will and Testament

I, _____ residing at _____ in the County of _____
_____, and State of _____, being of sound mind and memory, do make, publish and declare this to be my last Will and Testament, as follows, and hereby revoke any and all other former Wills made by me at any time.

First, The members of my immediate family are:

Name	Relationship	Address

Second, I order and direct that my just debts and funeral expenses, expenses for administration of my estate and any inheritance and succession taxes, state or federal, upon my estate shall be paid as soon after my death as may be practical.

Third, After my lawful debts are paid, I give all my estate to my wife/(husband)* In the event that my said wife/(husband)* shall predecease me or fails to survive me for sixty (60) days, I give all my estate to my children, adopted or afterborn as listed above, in equal shares, per stirpes. If I am survived by neither my wife nor my children, I give my estate to the following person or persons: _____ to be his/hers/theirs* in equal shares, or if not surviving, then to their children, if any, per stirpes.

Fourth, I nominate and appoint my wife/(husband)* as Guardian of my minor children and Executor/ Executrix* of this Will. In the event that my wife/(husband)* predeceases me, or fails to survive me or fails or is incapable to serve as Guardian or Executrix, then I nominate and appoint Mr/Mrs_____, as Guardian/co-Guardians of the persons and property of my minor child(ren), and Mr/Mrs_____ as substitute Executor/Executrix of my Will.

Fifth, I hereby authorize all my Executors/Executrixes and Guardians to exercise all the powers, rights, descretions, duties and immunities conferred upon fiduciaries to the extent permitted by law with full power to sell, lease, mortgage, invest, reinvest, or otherwise dispose of the assets of my estate, and all without posting bond and without court order.

---

*Delete the necessary word or term

𝕴𝖓 𝖂𝖎𝖙𝖓𝖊𝖘𝖘 𝖂𝖍𝖊𝖗𝖊𝖔𝖋 I have hereunto subscribed my name the _____ day of _____ 19_____.

SIGNED ✗ _____

(Testator's signature)

Attesting Witnesses

We, whose names are hereunto subscribed, DO CERTIFY that on the _____ day of _____ 19_____, the testator above named, subscribed his/her name to this instrument in our presence and in the presence of each of us, and at the same time, in our presence and to our hearing, the said testator declared the same to be his/her last Will and Testament, and requested us, and each of us, to sign our names thereto as witnesses to the execution thereof, which we hereby do in the presence of the testator(trix) and of each other, on the day of the date of the said Will.

SIGNED:

✗(1)_____ of _____
    (signature & name)   (City)   (State)

✗(2)_____ of _____
    (signature & name)   (City)   (State)

✗(3)_____ of _____
    (signature & name)   (City)   (State)

_____
*Every state requires at least two witnesses, some require three.

Chapter 6
THE LIVING WILL: HOW TO DRAFT ONE AND THE OTHER ESSENTIAL RELATED INSTRUMENTS THAT GO WITH IT

A. WHAT IS A LIVING WILL?

The living Will goes by different names in different states. Sometimes it's called a "Health Care Declaration," or a *"Medical Directive," "Directive to Physicians," "Durable Medical Power Of Attorney,"* or *"Durable Power Of Attorney For Health Care,"* and so on.

By whatever name it goes, however, the definition of the instrument is perhaps easier. Briefly defined, a Living Will is simply a written declaration by the living-Will maker (called the "declarant") by which the declarant directs that in the event he (or she) were to have a terminal condition or illness and such terminal condition or illness is of such nature that it is incurable or death is inevitable even if life-sustaining medical procedures are employed, then such procedures should not be employed merely to sustain or prolong his life. *The central intent which underlies the use of this instrument is simple: to allow the individual the free exercise of the right to die naturally — without unwarranted or unwanted medical interference.*

The "legislative" intent given by the California Legislature in the California Natural Death Act of 1976, the first Living Will law to be passed in the nation, pretty much sums up the rationale and objectives which commonly underlie the use of this instrument as an estate planning tool. It reads as follows:

> "…adult persons have the fundamental right to control the decisions relating to the tendering of their own medical care, including the decision to have life-sustaining procedures withheld or withdrawn in instances of terminal condition. …modern medical technology has made possible the artificial prolongation of human life beyond natural limits…[and] in the interest of protecting individual autonomy, such prolongation of life for persons with terminal condition may cause loss of patient dignity and unnecessary pain and suffering, while providing nothing medically necessary or beneficial to the patient…
>
> In recognition of the dignity and privacy which patients have a right to expect, the legislature hereby declares that the laws of the State of California shall recognize the right of an adult person to make a written directive instructing the physician to withhold or withdraw life-sustaining procedures in the event of terminal condition."

To put it simply, a living Will is a directive to direct doctors not to continue a prolonged "life support" medical treatment to keep you alive if, in their reasonable professional assessment, medical conditions clearly indicate there is no possibility of a return to a meaningful life. In recent years, the Living Will has come to be the primary legal device employed by individuals to lay down their wishes and desires regarding health care matters, use of life support equipment, and the like, and has therefore become a vital component in the overall estate planning scheme, as important, some estate planners say, as the traditional Will.

B. THE "COMPLETE" LIVING WILL PACKAGE: OTHER RELATED INSTRUMENTS YOU MUST HAVE ALONG WITH THE LIVING WILL

As can be expected, state laws on Living Wills vary widely. Many states require the use of a specific Living Will form, while many others do no. Many experts now contend, however, that most of the state laws on living wills, and most pre-printed Living Will forms provided under such state laws, are very limited in scope in terms of the medical and clinical conditions they cover, and give no room for liberal expression of one's own personal desires or preferences regarding use of life support devices or the kinds of medical treatment desired.[1] Hence, it is argued, it is constraining and inadequate to rely merely on the use of the state-mandated Living Will forms.

In the light of these considerations, we provide in this manual a system whereby you will be able to augment and complement a Living Will with two other related documents so as to constitute a "complete" Living Will package — the Durable Financial & Medical Power of Attorney, and the Medical Directive.

Hence, in the rest of this chapter, we shall address the preparation of the following documents which, together, will constitute a "complete" Living Will package:

- **THE LIVING WILL.** This document states the express intent of the maker (the 'declarant') that life-sustaining procedures not be employed if meaningful life is clearly impracticable or death is inevitable.
- **DURABLE FINANCIAL & MEDICAL POWER OF ATTORNEY.** This designates someone (called an "agent," a "proxy," or "Attorney-in-fact") to make decisions in regards to both financial and health care matters for the maker if, when, and during the time it's maker is incapacitated by reason of a physical or mental defect.
- **MEDICAL DIRECTIVE.** This serves as an aid to the appointed proxy or agent in clarifying and specifying exactly what kinds of medical treatments would be acceptable or not acceptable for you; it states your wishes regarding varying types of medical treatment in several representative situations. It will then be left to the person you appoint as your proxy decision-maker to make the decisions only in those circumstances where your situation is not exactly covered in the Medical Directive, or where your preference is undecided or unclear in the document.

Wills seem basic, but most people die without them.

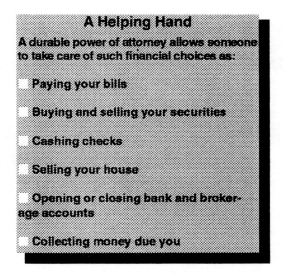

A Helping Hand

A durable power of attorney allows someone to take care of such financial choices as:

- Paying your bills
- Buying and selling your securities
- Cashing checks
- Selling your house
- Opening or closing bank and brokerage accounts
- Collecting money due you

C. NOW, LET'S DRAFT A LIVING WILL AND OTHER RELATED DOCUMENTS THAT GO WITH IT: THE STEP-BY-STEP PROCEDURES

To prepare and produce a valid Living Will and other essential companion instruments, simply follow the following procedures in the EXACT systematic order in which they are listed below:

---

[1]The primary argument cited by experts who contend that such a situation exists, include the following: that the Living Will forms only cover medical conditions classified as "terminal," as narrowly defined by state law; that Living Wills only apply to life support systems, and do not cover the health care decisions or personal desires regarding medical treatment; that in many states, Living Wills are valid only if signed after one has been informed that he or she has a "terminal" condition; and that a Living Will is generally addressed only to the doctors, and do not provide, for example, for appointment of someone to either make health care decisions for one or to see to it that one's wishes are, as expressed in fact, carried out. [See, for example, Alan D. Lieberson, The Living Will Handbook (Hastings House, Mamaroneck, NY, 1991), Section 2; and B.D. Colen, The Essential Guide To A Living Will (Prentice Hall, New York, 1991, esp. pp. ix-xii, 115-120.]

STEP ❶: PREPARE YOUR STATE'S STATUTORY FORM FOR LIVING WILL OR USE THE PUBLISHER'S GENERAL PURPOSE FORM

Refer to Appendix C (pp. 85-106), "Statutory And Other Living Will Forms For All 50 States."[2] These are the **statutory** Living Will forms under each state's living Will statutes (written law), but just for those states where it is mandatory under the state law that you must use the state-provided statutory form. Just pick out in Appendix C the Living Will form that applies for your state of residence or the state wherein your hospital is located or most likely to be located, and complete that form. Or, if your state does not mandate or require a specific "official" form (the relevant states that don't require specific forms are well indicated in Appendix C), then use the manual's *General Purpose Living Will Declaration* form listed on pp. 51-3, instead, in lieu of the state statutory form. (Leave out the signing aspect of the form for now, until you get to STEP 3 below.)

As of this writing, 5 states (Massachusetts, Michigan, Nebraska, Ohio and Pennsylvania) do not yet have specific Living Will statutes, but Massachusetts, Michigan, Ohio and Pennsylvania have statutory provisions for durable power of attorney for health care. And for any of these 5 states, you may employ the form on pp. 51-53. (If you happen to travel widely, or more frequently, or are likely to receive medical care in states other than the one in which you reside, it is advisable that you simply fill out and sign the statutory forms for each of those states as well. As far as is known, there is no law limiting the number of forms you may sign.)

Upon filling out the appropriate form in the manual for your state, do one of these two things: you may type out on a separate sheet the whole form with the details filled in, or, alternatively, simply send for a pre-printed Living Will form for your state from the organization listed below and then fill in the same information when you receive the pre-printed form from them. ***Here is where you may send for the pre-printed form:***

The National Council on Death & Dying
200 Varick Street
New York, N.Y. 10014

(It is supplied free of charge, but just enclose a self-addressed, stamped return envelope). Merely fill out the form for now, leave out the signing ("execution") part of the form for now till Step 3 below.

STEP ❷: COMPLETE THESE TWO ADDITIONAL FORMS: THE DURABLE FINANCIAL & MEDICAL POWER OF ATTORNEY, AND THE MEDICAL DIRECTIVE

NOTE: You may get a supply of the forms listed in this section from the Do-It-Yourself Legal Publishers. (See the Order Form on p. 124).

The sample form for the ***Durable Financial & Medical Power Of Attorney*** is on pp. 57-9; and the sample form for the ***Medical Directive*** is on pp.54-6. Note that you are only to fill out these forms for now, and leave out the actual signing ("execution") of the form till Step 3 below.

Basically, to complete the POWER OF ATTORNEY (pp. 57-9), the most important task of all for many people is to find the person who is to serve as the agent ("Attorney-in-Fact") to carry out the financial and health care wishes spelled out in the document. As in the naming of an executor in a Will situation or trust case, many people name trusted family members for that function (though there is no law that says you necessarily have

---

[2]It is possible that in the meantime your state may have revised the law and the specific forms contained in this manual, as has happened in some states in the last few years, usually to allow directives to discontinue therapy when the declarant is in a vergetative state, and to permit directives to withhold nutrition and hydration. Such revision, if made, do not invalidate or decrease the coverage of the pre-existing Will form or the directives therein, but often increase such coverage. However, if you wish to be able to take advantage of any new developments that may have arisen, it will be advisable to check with your state's county probate court clerk to see if any newer statutory form has come to use lately. Or, check with The National Council on Death & Dying in New York.

to). It should be noted, though, that this is one instance when you may consider designating a trusted friend or family member other than a spouse, in that the spouse is the person most likely to be in the company of an injured person and thus runs a greater risk of being involved in a common accident with you than others. [CLUE: Look for a person who knows you well enough, a person of compatible mind with you about what you consider a good "quality life," a person of honor and reliability, and one who is younger than you and in relative good health.]

Before you proceed to designate a person, be sure to fully explain to him (or her) the full ramifications of his potential responsibilities and be sure that he (she) unequivocally volunteers and agrees that he'll discharge such responsibilities on your behalf if the need should arise.

For the Power of Attorney, you (the principal) are to complete the first part of the form, while the person(s) you designate as your agent (also called the "attorney-in-fact" or the "proxy") is to complete the second part, the part captioned *"Affidavit of Agent as to Power of Attorney Being in Full Force."* The same person you enter as the designated agent or attorney-in-fact in your Power of Attorney form, is who you are also to enter as your agent in both the Living Will (if the state form you employ makes provisions for designation of an agent in the form) and also in the Medical Directive.

As to the filling out of the MEDICAL DIRECTIVE form (sample on pp. 54-6), the most vital aspect to concern yourself with is the making of a choice concerning the possible medical intervention you desire on each of the several situations outlined in that form.

There are 4 different situations of mental incompetence you are to consider:
i)   an irreversible coma or a persistent vegetative state (situation **A**);
ii) a coma with very slight and uncertain chance of recovery (situation **B**);
iii) irreversible brain damage or brain disease with a terminal illness (situation **C**); and
iv) irreversible brain damage or brain disease with no terminal illness (situation **D**).

For each of these 4 situations, you are to indicate your wish concerning the kind(s) of medical intervention you approve of, ranging from the giving of pain medications to resuscitation.

POINTER: First, discuss the issues, and the respective medical options and situations provided in the form, with your family, friends, religious mentors, and, lastly but quite importantly, with your doctor.

IMPORTANT: Be absolutely sure to COORDINATE the provisions of the Living Will with the provisions of the Durable Power of Attorney and the Medical Directive. The terms and provisions of these three documents must be CONSISTENT and not be conflicting. The same person(s) must be named as the agents in all three documents. In the MEDICAL DIRECTIVE you are to designate the name(s) of a person (or persons) who is to act as your agent or proxy decision-maker. This person would be the one who is to make decisions under circumstances in which your expressed wishes are not clear — when, for example, your specific situation is not covered in the Medical Directive or your preference is indeterminate or undecided. (Note that you can name more than one agent; if you do, just be sure to indciate whose opinion between them is to prevail in the event of a disagreement).

STEP ❸: NOW, STRICTLY FOLLOW THESE PROCEDURES TO "EXECUTE" OR SIGN THESE THREE DOCUMENTS

Now, this is the time for you (and some witnesses, in most cases) to formally sign — "execute" — the three above-described documents. To be sure that you'll have a valid set of instruments, *you MUST closely and strictly follow the following procedures in your signing act:*

1. You are to assemble the person(s) you have carefully picked who you will appoint to act as your agent or attorney-in-fact, and three (3) persons who will sign as witnesses to the signing event. *Any of these witnesses should <u>NOT</u>:*

 i) Be a minor under your state law (generally under 18)
 ii) Be related to you by blood or marriage or adoption
 iii) Be entitled to inherit from you under a Will or Codicil or under the law of intestate of your state
 iv) Have any claim against you or potentially have any claim against your estate
 v) Be your attending physician
 vi) Be a patient of the health care facility in which you are a patient or resident
 vii) Be an employee of your physician or of the health care facility in which you are being treated at the time of the signing of the Living Will
 viii) Be paid any compensation for acting as a witness
 ix) Have been the one who signed the Living Will itself for you, even if at your direction
 x) Have paid for you for your medical care
 xi) Be a person named in your Living Will or Power of Attorney as agent, proxy, or attorney-in-fact.[3]

2. NOW, WE COME TO THE ACTUAL SIGNING EVENT. You are, at this time, only to sign <u>two</u> of the three documents — THE LIVING WILL, AND THE MEDICAL DIRECTIVE. Now, with all the witnesses looking on, you should briefly inform the witnesses (and your would-be attorney-in-fact) that the document you have in front of you, about to sign, are two in number, and that they are your **Living Will** and your **Medical Directive.** (You may say something like: *"Gentlemen (Ladies), these two documents in front of me which I am about to sign, are: my Living Will, and my Medical Directive to Mr/Mrs_____, who I'm appointing to act as my agent for the Living Will. I have read these documents, and with sound mind and without pressure from anyone, I ask you to witness my signature, and to sign your own names after me as witnesses.")*

And with that statement, as the witnesses watch you, you initial and date <u>each</u> and <u>every</u> page of the Living Will and the Medical Directive documents at the top left-hand margin, and then sign your name in full on the last pages of each document. Sign in colored ink. (This way, the original document could be distinguishable) You sign all TWO documents. Fill in the date of the signing of each paper at the last page. (Sign only ONE original copy, but retain an unsigned copy.)

3. It will now be the turn of the witnesses, next, to sign. Ask each of the witnesses to read out loud the statement on the last page of the Living Will—the one just below your signature but above where the witnesses are supposed to sign, which says something about the witnesses not having any particular relationship with you. (Note that it is not necessary that the contents of the Living Will or the other documents be read or made known to the witnesses; in fact, it is advised against!).

 Then, as you watch each of the Witnesses, they will take turns to sign and enter their individual addresses in the spaces provided for them. They'll do this—that is, sign as witnesses—only on two of the documents— on the Living Will you have prepared, and on the Medical Directive (sample on p. 54). **The third document, the DURABLE POWER OF ATTORNEY, need not be signed by the witnesses.**

4. Finally, to complete the "execution" (the signing) phase, there's one more thing that needs to be done before you're done: getting the papers **notarized** by you and your witnesses and your appointed agents. Here's what you do. Just after the official signing ceremony, you should have your witnesses, as well as your agent or attorney-in-fact (all of them), stop by a Notary Public's office with the documents. This could be done on the same day of the Living Will signing affair; or later—but not too much later.

---

[3]NOTE: In South Carolina, the witness cannot be a physician, and if you are a patient in a hospital, or nursing or health care institution or facility in any of the states listed below, you should consider using as one of your witnesses, a patient embudsman, patient advocate, or the director of the medical facility: California, Delaware, District of Columbia, Georgia, Massachusetts, Michigan, Nebraska, New Hampshire, New Jersey, Ohio, Pennsylvania, Rhode Island, and South Dakota.

First, concerning the witnesses. In the presence of a Notary Public (he/she is generally located in most banks, real estate and lawyers offices, corner drug stores and the like), you yourself will first sign your name this time to only one document—the *LIVING WILL DECLARATION*. Then each of your 3 witnesses will sign their name after you on the paper. And the Notary Public will then "notarize" (i.e., stamp and sign) the document as confirmation that you and the witnesses did appear and sign the document in his presence. Thereafter, you should get the Declaration form back. It's now done.

And finally, it will now be the turn of the person you have picked to serve as your Attorney-in-fact (also called 'agent' of 'proxy' or 'decision-maker', etc.) to sign something. The agent is only to sign just one document — the second part of the Power of attorney document titled *"AFFIDAVIT OF AGENT AS TO POWER OF ATTORNEY BEING IN FULL FORCE"* (sample on p. 59). First of all, you yourself have to sign the Power of Attorney part (pp. 57-9) and notarize that part before the Notary Public. And thereafter the designated agent or agents will sign just the Affidavit of Agent part (p. 59) and have his or her own signature notarized by the Notary Public.

> **NOTE:** The value of the *Affidavit of Agent,* if and when it is signed by the appointed agent or attorney-in-fact, is that it serves as the agent's own word and legal assurance to outsiders that he was, in fact, granted the power of attorney and that the document still remains in force as of the time the agent is using or presenting it.

5. Have the needed number of copies of the documents made. Retain in your own records the original of the Living Will and copies of the Power of Attorney and Medical Directive. Give the originals of the Durable Power of Attorney and the Medical Directive, plus a copy of the Living Will, to your appointed attorney-in-fact (agent or proxy). Put the three documents in a thick envelope and seal it up with extra glue, and write these words on it: "The Living Will of ___(your name)___ and Related Documents." Then put away the envelope.

   Consider giving signed copies of all three documents, if appropriate for you, to the following parties: your family members, your attending or regular family physician (have him place a copy in your medical records file), your priest or pastor, and the executor of your Will. If you are a resident of a nursing home, give a copy to your nursing home director.

   When distributing copies, the location of the original (the copy that is signed in colored ink) should also be noted for the reason that it is only the presentation of the intact <u>original</u> that, to most people, will confirm that the documents continue to be valid.

> **NOTE:** For the Living Will to remain valid, California requires that you re-sign it (you have to go through the whole signing and witnessing formalities over again) every 5 years, while Georgia requires that you do so every 7 years.

D. HOW TO REVOKE YOUR LIVING WILL AND/OR DURABLE POWER OF ATTORNEY

Occasions may well arise when you'll want to change your Living Will and/or the related documents, or to even totally revoke them. There are any number of circumstances which could conceivably warrant that, as it is not unusual to find, with the passage of time, many changes occurring in one's conditions, attitudes and position. It is not uncommon to find, for example, that persons who are designated attorneys-in-fact or proxies may at some point not be available to serve by reason of death, relocation, change of mind, etc. Furthermore, persons appointed to act as attorneys-in-fact in a Living Will or Medical Power of Attorney situation may, at times, have second thoughts about it and may request to be removed, and so on.

In any event, if for whatever reason you should want or need to change or revoke your Living Will or Financial/Medical Power of Attorney, there are specific procedures you must follow for it to be legal and valid: In the first instance, you should know that a Living Will (or Power of Attorney) may be revoked at any time by the declarant or maker, without regard to his (her) mental state or competence. This may be done by any one of the following methods: by destruction of the document (the original); by written revocation; and by verbal expression of revocation.

Revocation by written revocation is the most common and more generally accepted method used. *Follow this simple procedure:*

1. Complete this form: ***Revocation Of Living Will and Durable Financial & Medical Power of Attorney, And the Notice thereof (sample copy on p. 60).***
2. Properly sign, date and <u>notarize</u> this document.
3. Make several photocopies of the document. Then distribute these copies (preferably, send them by certified mail, with return receipt requested) to all interested parties in your situation — to each and every person designated in your Living Will and in the Power of Attorney, including the wistnesses, and certainly your proxy or attorney-in-fact, the family physician, any other persons you or your proxy may have given a copy of the documents to, etc.

Under the law of most states, revocation is effective when and once it is communicated to a party; and a party who nevertheless goes ahead and utilizes or relies on the underlying document upon being notified or made aware of the revocation, is subject to both civil and criminal liabilities.

The Living Will Declaration *[The Publisher's General Purpose Form]*

OF _____

To my Family, Doctors, Authorized Agents, and all those concerned with my health care:

I, _____, resident at_____, being of sound mind, witfully and voluntarily declare my desire that my life not be artificially prolonged under the circumstances set forth below, and, pursuant to all applicable laws, both statutory and common, in the state listed below or wherein I may become incapacitated, I declare that:

1. If at any time I should have been diagnosed as being in a persistent vegetative state or should have an incurable injury, disease, or illness which causes me severe distress and/or unconsciousness and has been certified to be a terminal condition by two (2) physicians who have both personally examined me, one of whom is my attending physician, and the physicians have determined that there can be no recovery from such condition and/or that death will occur therefrom without the administration of life-sustaining procedures, and if in the professional opinion of the said two physicians the application of life-sustaining procedures would serve only to artificially prolong the dying process, I direct that in such event such procedures or treatment be withheld or withdrawn and that I be permitted to die naturally with only the administration of medication , food or fluid or the performance of medical procedures deemed necessary to provide me with comfort or to alleviate pain.

   In short, if I should at any time be in an incurable or irreversible mental or physical condition and my physicians have, upon examination, duly certified that in their professional opinion there is no reasonable expectation of my recovery therefrom, or of regaining conciousness and meaningful state of health, I direct my attending physician(s) to withhold or withdraw treatment that merely prolongs my dying, and direct that treatment be limited only to measures to keep me comfortable and to relieve pain.

2. If I should become unable to give directions regarding my treatment or the use of life sustaining procedures in the above situations, it is my wish and expectation that my family, doctors, or my designated agent, if any, and any court of law, shall honor and be morally and legally bound by this Declaration, EXCEPT that all such persons and their actions shall always be guided in such an instance by the directives contained in the 3-page document executed by me and titled *"THE MEDICAL DIRECTIVE,"* which is annexed hereto.

3. If I should become physically or mentally unable to communicate my instructions as stated in this Declaration, I designate and authorize the following person or persons, namely Mr/Mrs_____ of _____, to act in my behalf as my primary proxy. The said person or persons are also named in a separate written instrument titled DURABLE FINANCIAL & MEDICAL POWER OF ATTORNEY, and are to act in my behalf as my agent or attorney-in-fact thereof in accordance with the provisions therein, and of the ← (Medical Directive.

4. No person or entity, whether designated in this Declaration or otherwise, or the attending physician, health care institution or licensed health care professional, shall incur any legal or moral liabilities of any nature whatsoever for following or carrying out in good faith my directions in this Declaration.

5. If I am diagnosed, however, as pregnant, this Declaration shall have no force and effect or be operative during the course of my pregnancy.

6. This Declaration may be revoked by me, the Declarant, at any time, without regard to my physical or mental condition, by: (a) being defaced, torn, obliterated, or otherwise destroyed by me or by someone else in my presence and at my direction; (b) either a written revocation signed and dated by me, or by verbal revocation by me duly communicated to the attending physician by me, expressing my intent to revoke the declaration.

In Witness Whereof, I, the undersigned Declarant, do hereby make and sign this Living Will Declaration consisting of _____ typewritten (or handwritten) pages, on the date hereinafter entered, and declare that I do so with a full and competent understanding as to its meaning, consequence, and impact, and that I am of sound mind and legal age and under no constraint or undue influence whatsoever.

DATED:_____   SIGNED: ✗_____

(Declarant, or person signing for him/her, if applicable)

AT:_____   NAME (print):_____
(town/city)   (state)

Statement By The Witnesses (To The Living Will)

We, the witnesses whose names are signed below, do hereby declare that on _____ 19____, and in the presence of all of us, the above-named Declarant did sign the foregoing instrument designated as his/her LIVING WILL DECLARATION, and that thereupon, at the said Declarant's request and in his (her) presence, and in each other's presence, we signed our names below as witnesses, and further declare individually and severally under the penalty of perjury, that, to the best of our knowledge, the following are true:

1. The Declarant is personally known to us and we believe the Declarant to be at least 18 years of age and of sound mind.
2. Each of us is at least 18 years of age.
3. To the best of our knowledge, at the time of the execution of this Living Will Declaration, anyone of us:
   a) is not related to the Declarant by blood or marriage;
   b) would not be entitled to any portion of the Declarant's estate by any Will or by operation of law under the rules of descent and distribution of this state;
   c) is not the attending physician of the Declarant or an employer of the attending physician or an employee of the hospital or skilled nursing facility in which the Declarant is a patient;
   d) is not directly financially responsible for the Declarant's medical care; and
   e) has no present claim against any portion of the estate of the Declarant.
4. We all witnessed the execution of the within Living Will Declaration by the within named Declarant (or the signer for an oral declarant).
5. The said Declarant subscribed to and signed the said LIVING WILL DECLARATION and declared it to be his/her Living Will in our presence.
6. We thereafter subscribed to and signed the said document as witnesses, in the presence of the said Declarant, and in the presence of each other and at the request of the said Declarant.
7. We make this affidavit at the request of the said Declarant, _____
   (Declarant's name)
8. The Declarant fully appeared to us to have signed the said instrument freely and under no apparent constraint or undue influence, and was fully aware of the meaning and import of the action.

Witnesses sign here indicating their residency:

X_____residing at_____
(Town or City/State)

X_____residing at_____

X_____residing at_____

[Witnesses (and party signing for oral declarant, if applicable) shall also sign as follows in the form of an affidavit before a Notary Public]

STATE OF_____)ss:
COUNTY OF_____)

Then and there personally appeared before me, a duly authorized notary public in and for the county and state above captioned, the within named persons, now listed as follows:

_____, _____, _____
[name of first witness]   [second witness]   [third witness]

and   _[the declarant or signer of Oral Declaration for Declarant, if any]_ ,who being duly sworn, individually depose, attest and acknowledge:

That, in the presence of all the witnesses, the Declarant did sign the above Living Will Declaration; that at the Declarant's request, and in the presence of the Declarant and of each other, each of the witnesses signed as witnesses; that, to the best of their knowledge, the Declarant did sign the said Living Will Declaration freely, under no constraint or undue influence, and was of sound mind and memory and legal age, and fully aware of the meaning and import of this action; and that this affidavit is made by the witnesses at the direction of and in the presence of the Declarant.

SUBSCRIBED AND SWORN TO BEFORE ME   Seal:
this_____day of_____19_____.   (Notary Public)

_____
      (Notary Public)

(If this Declaration is signed in a nursing home or other extended care facility, the additional witness designated below should sign below as well)

I hereby witness this Living Will and attest that I believe the Declarant to be of sound mind and to have made this Living Will Declaration willingly and voluntarily.

Witness ✗_____*

---

*Medical director of skilled nursing facility or staff physician not participating in care of the patient or chief of the health care facility.

The Medical Directive Of Mr/Mrs_____

MY MEDICAL DIRECTIVE	SITUATION A	SITUATION B

MY MEDICAL DIRECTIVE

This Medical Directive expresses, and shall stand for, my wishes regarding medical treatments in the event that illness should make me unable to communicate them directly. I make this Directive, being 18 years or more of age, of sound mind, and appreciating the consequences of my decisions.

SITUATION A

If I am in a coma or a persistent vegetative state and, in the opinion of my physician and several consultants, have no known hope of regaining awareness and higher mental functions no matter what is done, then my wishes regarding use of the following, if considered medically reasonable, would be:

X_____
(signature)

SITUATION B

If I am in a coma and, in the opinion of my physician and several consultants, have a small likelihood of recovering fully, a slightly larger likelihood of surviving with permanent brain damage, and a much larger likelihood of dying, then my wishes regarding use of the following, if considered medically reasonable, would be:

My Full Name_____
(Principal)

Treatment	I want	I want treatment tried. If no clear improvement, stop.	I am undecided	I do not want	I want	I want treatment tried. If no clear improvement, stop.	I am undecided	I do not want
Cardiopulmonary Resuscitation: if at the point of death, using drugs and electric shock to keep the heart beating; artificial breathing.		Not applicable				Not applicable		
Mechanical Breathing: breathing by machine.								
Artificial Nutrition and Hydration: giving nutrition and fluid through a tube in the veins, nose, or stomach.								
Major Surgery, such as removing the gall bladder or part of the intestines.		Not applicable				Not applicable		
Kidney Dialysis: cleaning the blood by machine or by fluid passed through the belly.								
Chemotherapy: using drugs to fight cancer.								
Minor Surgery, such as removing some tissue from an infected toe.		Not applicable				Not applicable		
Invasive Diagnostic Tests, such as using a flexible tube to look into the stomach.		Not applicable				Not applicable		
Blood or Blood Products, such as giving transfusions.								
Antibiotics: using drugs to fight infection.								
Simple Diagnostic Tests, such as performing blood tests or x-rays.		Not applicable				Not applicable		
Pain Medications, even if they dull consciousness and indirectly shorten my life.		Not applicable				Not applicable		

Page 1 of 3 Pages

The Medical Directive of_____cont'd

SITUATION C

If I have brain damage or some brain disease that in the opinion of my physician and several consultants cannot be reversed and that makes me unable to recognize people or to speak understandably, *and I also have a terminal illness,* such as incurable cancer, that will likely be the cause of my death, then my wishes regarding use of the following, if considered medically reasonable, would be:

SITUATION D

If I have brain damage or some brain disease that in the opinion of my physician and several consultants cannot be reversed and that makes me unable to recognize people or to speak understandably, *but I have no terminal illness, and I can live in this condition for a long time,* then my wishes regarding use of the following, if considered medically reasonable, would be:

My Full Name_____
(Principal)

_____
(signature)

I want	I want treatment tried. If no clear improvement, stop.	I am undecided	I do not want
	Not applicable		
	Not applicable		
	Not applicable		
	Not applicable		
	Not applicable		

I want	I want treatment tried. If no clear improvement, stop.	I am undecided	I do not want
	Not applicable		
	Not applicable		
	Not applicable		
	Not applicable		
	Not applicable		

The Medical Directive Of_____ cont'd

I understand that my wishes expressed in these four cases may not cover all possible aspects of my care if I become incompetent. I also may be undecided about whether I want a particular treatment or not. Consequently, there may be a need for someone to accept or refuse medical interventions for me in consultation with my physicians. I authorize

1. *[enter name of your first agent, who is to act on your behalf]* _____

2. *[enter name of your appointed 2nd agent]* _____

as my proxy(s) to make the decision for me whenever my wishes expressed in this document are insufficient or undecided.

Should there be any disagreement between the wishes I have indicated in this document and the decision favored by my above-named proxy(s),
(Please delete one of the following two lines.)

I wish my proxy(s) to have authority over my Medical Directive.
(or)
I wish my Medical Directive to have authority over my proxy(s).

Should there be any disagreement between the wishes of my proxies,

_____ *[enter name of the preferred agent]* _____ . shall have final authority.

ORGAN DONATION

I hereby make this anatomical gift to take effect upon my death.   *[If not filled in, then CROSS OUT completely]*
(Please check boxes and fill in blanks where appropriate.)

I give
☐ my body;   ☐ any needed organs or parts;
☐ the following organs or parts _____
_____

to
☐ the following person or institution: _____
_____ ;
☐ the physician in attendance at my death;
☐ the hospital in which I die;
☐ the following named physician, hospital, storage bank, or other medical institution: _____
_____

for the following purposes:
☐ any purpose authorized by law;   ☐ transplantation;
☐ therapy of another person;   ☐ research;
☐ medical education.

MY PERSONAL STATEMENT (use another page if necessary)

_____

_____

Signed ✗ *[you sign your name here & enter date]*   Date_____

Witness ✗ *[1st witness signs here & enters date]*   Date_____

Witness ✗ *[For 2nd witness & date]*   Date_____

Witness ✗ *[For 3rd witness & date]*   Date_____

Durable Financial & Medical Power of Attorney

Know all Men by these Presents,

That I, _____, as the principal, residing at _____,
do hereby designate and appoint, Mr/Mrs/Ms:_____, presently at this
address_____, as my true and lawful Agent and Attorney-in-Fact, for the purpose of
making financial decisions, and/or medical and health care decisions on my behalf if, DURING and owing to a
condition resulting from illness or injury, I am deemed by my attending physician(s) to be incapable to make
such decisions or to be incapable to competently or knowingly authorize or approve such decisions by reason
of a physical or mental disability, incompetence or incapacitation.

Pursuant to this, I HEREBY authorize my above-named Attorney-in-Fact as follows, on the following two-part matters:*

A. Financial Affairs Decisions

(1) To enter upon and take possession of any lands, tenements and hereditaments that may belong to
me, or to the possession of which I may be entitled;

(2) To ask for, collect and receive any rents, profits, issues or income of any and all of such lands, tenements and hereditaments, or of any part or parts thereof;

(3) To pay any and all taxes, charges and assessments that may be levied, assessed or imposed upon
any of my lands, buildings, tenements or other structures;

(4) To make, execute and deliver any deed, mortgage or lease, whether with or without covenants and
warranties, in respect of any such lands, tenements and hereditaments, or of any part or parts thereof, and to
manage, repair, rebuild or reconstruct any buildings, houses or other structures or any part or parts thereof, that
may now or hereafter be owned by me or be erected upon any such lands;

(5) To extend, renew, replace or increase any mortgage(s) now or hereafter affecting any of my lands,
tenements and hereditaments and/or any personal property belonging to me, and, for any such purposes, to
sign, seal, acknowledge and deliver any bond or bonds, or to make, sign and deliver any note or notes, or any
extension, renewal, consolidation or apportionment agreement or agreements, or any other instrument, whether
sealed or unsealed, that may be useful or necessary to accomplish any of the foregoing purposes;

(6) To obtain insurance (and other similar instruments) of any kind, nature or description whatsoever, on
any of my lands, tenements and hereditaments and/or in connection with the management, use or occupation
thereof and/or on any personal property belonging to me and/or in respect of the rents, issues and profits arising therefrom, and to make, execute and file proof(s) of all losse(s) sustained or claimable thereunder, and to
make, and execute receipts, releases or other discharges therefor.

(7) To demand, sue for, collect, recover and receive all goods, claims, debts, monies, interests and
demands whatsoever now due, or that may hereafter be due or belong to me (including the right to institute any
action, suit or legal proceeding for the recovery of any land, buildings, tenements or other structures, or any part
(s)thereof, to the possession whereof I may be entitled) and to make and execute receipts, releases or other discharges therefor, for them.

(8) To make, execute, endorse, accept, collect and deliver any or all bills of exchange, checks, drafts,
notes and trade acceptances;

---

*For any clause(s) or provision(s) not desired, completely delete same, but adequately initial them.

(9) To pay all sums of money that may hereafter be owing by me on any bill of exchange, check, draft, note or trade acceptance, made, or executed by me or for me, and in my name, by my said attorney;

(10) To make gifts, which shall in no event be more than $10,000, to each person per year ($20,000 to each marital couple, if applicable), to my lawful children (and spouse), if I have previously been in the pattern of making such gifts, and/or at the good faith discretion of the attorney-in-fact that such gifts are warranted for estate planning or other purposes and are affordable by my estate.

(11) To sell, mortgage or hypothecate any and all shares of stock, bonds or other securities now or hereafter belonging to me; and to make, execute and deliver assignment(s) of any such shares of stock, bonds or other securities, either absolutely or as collateral security.

(12) To defend, settle, adjust, compound, submit to arbitration and compromise all actions, suits, accounts, reckonings, claims and demands whatsoever that now are, or hereafter shall be pending between me and any personor entity in such a manner as my said attorney shall think fit;

(13) To file any proof of claim or of debt, or take any other proceedings, under the Bankruptcy Act, or under any law of any state or territory of the United States, in connection with any such claim, debt, money or demand, and to represent me in all respects in any such proceeding or proceedings, and to demand, receive and accept any dividend or dividends, or distribution or distributions that may be or become payable thereunder;

(14) To hire accountants, financial professionals, real estate agents, attorneys at law, clerks, workmen and others, and to remove them, and appoint others in their place, and to pay and allow to the persons to be so employed such salaries, wages or other renumerations, as my said attorney shall think fit;

(15) To constitute and appoint, in his place and stead, and as his substitute, one or more attorney-in-fact, for me, with full power of revocation; and

(16) _____

(describe here any other or additional authority you wish not previously mentioned above)

_____

B. Medical Care Decisions

(17) To consent, refuse to consent, withdraw consent, to any care, treatment, service, or procedure to maintain, diagnose, or treat my physical or mental condition.

(18) To inspect and disclose any information relating to my physical and mental health or condition.

(19) To sign documents, waivers, and releases, including documents titled or purporting to be a "Refusal to Permit Treatment" and "Leaving the Hospital or Refusing Treatment Against Medical Advice", and to execute any waiver or release from liability required by a hospital, medical institution or physician.

(20) In general, to act in accordance with and in conformity to the directives in the 3-page document titled "THE MEDICAL DIRECTIVE" which is executed by me and annexed hereto. The agent's decisions shall be overriden by my wishes in the DIRECTIVE whenever there is or appears to be a conflict in our positions.

(21) I DECLARE that this Power of Attorney, in its entirety, and its validity or operation thereof, shall not be affected by my subsequent disability, incompetence or incapacity as recognized unde the applicable state laws, and that the authority granted herein shall continue and remain in full force and effect in the event that I become, and during any period while I am disabled, incompetent or incapacitated, unless sooner revoked or terminated by me in writing.

(22) The foregoing power and authority granted herein are herewith granted without, in any way, limiting the said appointed Agent, generally to do, execute and perform any other act, deed, mater or thing whatsoever, that ought to be done, executed and performed, or that, in the opinion of my said agent or attorney-in-fact ought to be done, executed or performed, in and about my premises, financial affairs, medical treatment, or health care, of every nature and kind whatsoever consistent with my directives, as fully effectual as I could do if personally present.

(23) And I do hereby ratify and confirm all things whatsoever that my said attorney-in-fact or his subsitute or substitutes, shall do, or cause to be done, in or about the premises, and my affairs, by virtue of this power of attorney.

(24) This instrument may not be changed orally.

(25) If the first person I named above is unavailable to act as the agent or attorney-in-fact in my behalf, I hereby authorize the following person(s) _____,
        (Name)   (Address)
as the substitute agent(s) or attorney-in fact with the same powers, authority and responsibilities.

𝕴𝖓 𝖂𝖎𝖙𝖓𝖊𝖘𝖘 𝖂𝖍𝖊𝖗𝖊𝖔𝖋, I have hereunto set my hand and seal the _____ day of _____19_____.

SIGNED X:_____
                                    (The Principal)

Acknowledgment

STATE OF_____ }
COUNTY OF_____ } ss.:
On the_____day of_____19____ before me personally came Mr/Mrs_____,
to me known or made known to me to be the individual described in, the foregoing POWER OF ATTORNEY, and who, upon first being duly sworn executed the said POWER OF ATTORNEY, and thereupon acknowledged to me under oath that __he executed the same.

_____
(Notary Public)

Affidavit Of Agent As To Power Of Attorney Being In Full Force

(Attach to The power of Attorney)

STATE OF_____ }
COUNTY OF_____ } ss.:
Mr/Mrs/Ms _____, being duly sworn, deposes and says under the penalty of perjury:
        [agent enters his/her name]

That _____ as principal, who resides at _____
        [Your name is entered here]   *[your address]*
did, in writing, on the date of _____,appoint me as his true and lawful Agent and
                                [date when the Power of Attorney was signed]
Attorney-in-fact, and that annexed hereto, and hereby made a part thereof, is a true copy of the said Power Of Attorney.

THAT, as agent and attorney-in-fact of the said principal, and under and by virtue of the said power of attorney, I have this day executed the following described instrument(s):

[Enter any papers or documents you might be signing or presenting here in furtherance of your function as agent in this capacity]

THAT I hereby represent that the said principal is now alive; that at the time of the granting of this instrument __he is of sound mind; that __he has not, at any time, revoked or repudiated the said power of attorney; and that the said power of attorney is in current and full force and effect.

That I make this affidavit for the purpose of inducing any party, person or entity in interest to accept delivery of the above described instrument, as executed by me in my capacity as attorney-in-fact of the said principal, with the full knowledge that if in accepting the execution and delivery of the aforesaid instrument, and/or in paying a good and valuable consideration therefor, the said party or entity herein being induced, will rely upon this affidavit.

Sworn to before me

this _____day of_____19___   Signed X_____
                                                                        (Attorney-in-Fact/Agent)
_____
Notary Public

_____
NOTE: This AFFIDAVIT part is to be filled in and notarized by the person appointed to act for you as your Attorney-in-Fact (agent), and not by you, the Principal.

Revocation Of Living Will and Durable Financial & Medical Power of Attorney, And The Notice Thereof

Know all Men by these Presents,

1. That on the date(s) hereinafter listed alongside each document, I, Mrs/Mrs_____, the undersigned, did execute the following document(s):

(Check (✔) off the appropriate one or ones)

☐ The Living Will Declaration   Date when executed:_____

☐ The Medical Directive   Date when executed:_____

☐ Durable Financial & Medical Power of Attorney   Date when executed:_____

2. That as Declarant and Principal of the said instrument(s), I did designate and appoint therein, Mr/Mrs/Ms_____, as my agent, proxy and attorney-in-fact in the said instrument(s) for the purpose of making financial decisions and/or medical and health care decisions on my behalf in certain times and under conditions of mental or physical incapacitation specified therein.

3. Whereupon BY THESE PRESENTS, I DO HEREBY REVOKE, CANCEL AND VOID the above checked and described document(s), and all of the powers and authorities given therein, effective immediately.

Dated this_____day of_____19____.

SIGNED: **✗**_____
                                 (signature—Declarant)

_____
                                 (Address)

_____
                           (City/State/Zip Code)

Acknowledgment

STATE OF_____)
) ss.
COUNTY OF_____)

On this_____day of_____19____, before me, the undersigned Notary Public, personally appeared Mr/Mrs/Ms_____, to me known or made known to me to be the individual described in and who executed under oath the foregoing *Revocation of Living Will and Durable Financial & Medical Power Of Attorney,* and acknowledged that he(she) executed the same as his (her) free act and deed.

My Commission expires:_____   _____
                                                       (Notary Public)

Chapter 7

HOW TO MAKE YOUR WILL CHALLENGE-PROOF IN PROBATE: THE "PITFALLS" TO AVOID IN DRAFTING YOUR WILL

MAKING YOUR WILL CHALLENGE-PROOF

In the overwhelming majority of cases, the terms and provisions of the Will which is presented for probate are generally acceptable to the court and to all parties in interest as valid and final; and no challenge is mounted against the Will. [See p. 112]. As might perhaps be expected, there are still a tiny number of cases, however, when Wills — regardless of who drafted them, whether they be lawyers or non-lawyers — are open to challenges and a contest. *What can you do to ensure not only that your Will is legally valid, but that it is "challenge-proof" — i.e., that it will withstand any possible challenge or contest in court by relatives and any parties in interest?* THE SIMPLE ANSWER IS: QUITE A LOT!!!

HERE ARE THE TYPICAL "PITFALLS" TO AVOID

Expert estate planners and court judges[1] point to a host of "pitfalls" in Will-drafting, almost all of which are actually undertaken by lawyers, which cause probate problems and litigations over Wills. And analysts maintain that if such pitfalls could be avoided in the drafting of a Will, it would not only drastically reduce or eliminate such probate problems and court challenges and litigation against Wills, but that it would save the heirs a lot of expense and grief later on down the road.

The following, based on the author's research, are substantially the major pitfalls you must avoid in the drafting of a Will. *Taken together, these constitute the basic pitfalls which, if you can avoid, will almost guarantee that the Will you produce is not only going to be legally valid, but that it will best safeguard the interests of the Will-maker and his/her heirs while being almost unassailable and challenge-proof in court:*

1. If you rearrange trust funds and shift assets (as a tax saving or estate planning device, perhaps), you must immediately update your Will or have a new one written. Make it a habit to dutifully review your Will periodically (say, every 4 or 5 years) and write a new Will or amendment ("codicil") to take into account continuing changes in your life [See pp. 39-40 for more on this].

2. If and whenever you make and sign a new Will, you should immediately and actually destroy the old, pre-existing one. [If you leave both the new and old ones around, there's always the possibility that only the first one will be found, or that a disinherited or unscrupulous heir may destroy the later one, and the first one will stand as your final Will!]

3. Whenever you review your Will, you must always do so side-by-side with all the other major estate planning instruments you have (Trusts, Living Will, Insurance Plans, Jointly held accounts or property, etc...), in order to make absolutely certain that the provisions of all instruments are thoroughly **coordinated** and **compatible** with the provisions of the Will. A common example of the way this mistake works

---

[1]See, for example, "Your Money: Many Advised To Review Wills," N.Y. Times, Oct. 14, 1989, p. 34.

among Will-drafters, is for the Will writer to include a debt payment or a "tax-exoneration clause" — a provision directing that all taxes and/or debts of the testator be paid from the "residuary estate" — in both the Will and the Trust, which then results in the court having to be brought in to decide what to do. Or, a testator may designate a specific beneficiary in a financial instrument, such as a life insurance, which is different from the one he or she shall have named as the beneficiary in the Will or the one which he/she has in mind when he assigned certain debt payment or gift-giving obligations to his "residuary estate"[2] in the Will [see, for example, Appendix D, Section D, at p. 109, for more on this.]

4. If you have minor children, you should first consult very closely with the people you choose to serve as guardians for your children and first get their agreement before you proceed to name them as guardians in your Will. Give detailed thought and consideration to who would be best qualified to look after the children. Seek to pick persons with a similar view of the world as you, a contemporary rather than just one of your parents. [If, say, the guardian has a small home, you could consider providing money in your Will so that the guardian may buy a larger home to comfortably accommodate your children.]

5. The trustee or guardian of your children's "property" (money, etc...) may, if you prefer and have good reason for it, be a separate person from the trustee or guardian of their "person." [Aunt Angie may be the logical one to raise the children, but you don't feel she could properly manage the cash and/or property. In that event, you may consider someone else, or a bank, to be the guardian of the property. Bear in mind, though, that these two parties will have to be able to consult and get along or work with each other for this arrangement to work.]

6. In the "execution" (the signing) part of your Will, always try to use MORE than the number of witnesses stipulated under your state's law. (That means, essentially, that for most states, you should use at least 3 witnesses.) Also, try to get witnesses that are younger than the testator and in relative good health, at least ones who aren't elderly. In addition to their present addresses, a record should be made (by the testator) of the immediate relatives or friends of the witnesses through whom the said witnesses may be located if they were to change addresses or move from the state. Don't just call somebody in off the street as a witness, unless you have no alternative; try to have as witnesses people you know, and who will be available, if needed.

7. Use good bond paper for writing the original Will. Never, REPEAT, NEVER execute a zerox copy as the original. Never use treated paper as the original. It is alright to zerox the <u>unexecuted</u> original for use in conformed copies, ***but never allow the original Will, after execution, to be zeroxed.*** USE COLORED INK, RATHER THAN BLACK INK, TO SIGN THE WILL so as to differentiate the original from any photocopies.

8. As to the actual wording of the Will, use simple language. Avoid the lawyers' typical jargon, such as "per stirpes," "per capita," etc. Spell out the distributions in detail and in specifics.

9. Be clear and simple. Avoid ambiguity. A good test is this: Re-read a paragraph. If it is open to more than one interpretation, rewrite it. Then, re-read it again—until you're finally sure it's clear and unambiguous.

10. Make sure ALL assets are distributed. (Make an itemized, comprehensive listing of all "probate estate" types of assets—i.e., those that you really own and are subject to distribution (see pp. 3, 18-23 & 109)). If you are using percentages, check to see that all legacies added together total exactly 100%.

---

[2]Funds held, for example, in a bank account in trust for another person cannot be left to a third person unless the Will specifically revokes that trust and names the institution where the account is held.

11. In appointing Executors and/or Trustees or guardians, the provision not to require them to post a bond should never be omitted (unless, however, the testator actually desires bonded fiduciaries). (In the case of a Trustee, failure in the Will to make any reference to a bond will almost surely mandate that he be required to post one even if the testator wishes otherwise.)

12. If you pick a trusted relative to act as your estate's executor (the usual practice by most persons), make sure he's at least financially responsible, that he's not the type who will readily be tempted to "borrow" from the estate assets. Having some business experience and financial management experience will be helpful. *If he's economically broke and short of money, if you have the slightest qualms about the reli ability of the relative you're considering, do this: either reject him outright, or, if you can't because he's the only viable option, expressly provide in the Will for him to serve under a bond* (posting a bond with the court guarantees that if the executor were to run off with the money, the estate will be reimbursed for it. However, note that there's a charge to be paid out of your estate assets to get the bonding.)

13. Provide for the appointment of alternate or successor executors and/or successor trustees and guardians.

14. Give the executor broad discretionary powers to resolve conflicts and settle disputed issues, especially matters like distribution of household effects and personal property. In general, give your executors detailed, broad fiduciary powers to deal with any contingencies, foreseeable and anticipated. ***This is one major way to avert a common basis for challenges to a Will.***

15. Exercise foresight. Anticipate possible changes. For example, in case a named charity or beneficiary (or for that matter, a named executor, trustee, etc..) ceases to exist or dies or is for any reason unavailable, give a second choice, and perhaps a third choice.

16. Expressly specify in the Will whether specified or given assets are to·be distributed by "fractional" or by "pecuniary" method. [Generally courts will interpret words like "sum" or "amount" to be pecuniary, and words like "percentage" or "part" to be fractional.]

17. When it comes to actual execution of the Will, establish a routine set of formalities and "ceremonies" and stick strictly to them—they should be ones that will impress the witnesses and remain "sticking out" in their memory. [See pp. 37, 41].

18. It is always a very good procedure to have the witnesses execute as well, a self-proving affidavit [see p. 38]. Have it done at the time of the original execution. Choose a good form, one that fully complies with statutory requirements for execution.

19. After the execution of the Will, thereafter, absolutely no changes or modification of any kind should be made on the original instrument—unless you completely repeat the whole formal drafting and signing procedure. (Many testators who have possession of the original Will would often make changes in them in amounts and names. It usually happens when a legatee has died or after a serious disagreement with a legatee. This is absolutely not permitted).

20. Include a pedigree or family tree in the Will. This will save time in probate in sorting out family relationships.

21. Specify burial and funeral preferences in the Will, including whether you want to be buried or cremated.

22. If you and your spouse provide for reciprocal bequests to each other (i.e., each leaving his/her estate to the other) and then go on to provide that if you both die simultaneously in a common disaster the estates are to be distributed to named beneficiaries, remember to direct the distribution of the estate of the second spouse to die, since the more likely scenario is that both spouses will probably not die simultaneously.

23. Separately maintain a memo and an itemized list and instructions to aid your executor in his task in the event he or she more suddenly called upon to act; attach a copy of this memo to your original Will. [See sample of this in Appendix B on pp. 79-84]. Attempt to update it periodically, as frequently as necessary.

24. In general, try to avoid the "don'ts" specified in Section K of Chapter 2 [p. 15] and to comply with the dictates set forth in Section M of Chapter 2 [p. 16].

The suggestions made herein are, it should be noted, more "practical" than "legal." However, if they are faithfully followed, they will help immensely to eliminate many legal problems in the future probate of your Will in particular, and the administration of your estate, in general. ***In deed, if these rules were to be strictly observed, it is almost GUARANTEED that the will you come up with shall have been as "challenge-proof" as any human, a lawyer or non-lawyer, can ever make it!***

Chapter **8**
Your Will And Estate Taxes: Is So-Called 'Tax Planning' Really Relevant For You In Making Your Will?

A. THE (NEW) REALITIES ABOUT ESTATE TAX SAVINGS THROUGH SOME PLANNING GIMMICKRY: YOU MAY NOT HAVE A BIG ENOUGH ESTATE

To begin with, let's get one fundamental point clear outright: CHANCES ARE THAT YOU MAY NOT HAVE AN ESTATE TAX 'PROBLEM' IN THE FIRST PLACE; ONLY IF YOU FALL WITHIN THAT TINY PROPORTION OF ALL ESTATES WHICH COMES WITHIN THE SOCIETY'S UPPERMOST WEALTH BRACKET, SHOULD YOU ACTIVELY AND ACTUALLY BEGIN TO WORRY!

Traditionally, lawyers would give you a big argument contending that one "major pitfall" why non-lawyers should never even attempt to draft their own wills or trusts (but should, of course, pay a lawyer to do it!), is that a non-lawyer would need to be skilled in the ins and outs of working the maximum possible estate "tax savings" into his self-made Will!! This has been the lawyer's claim historically.[1] It so happens, though, that like all such claims by tradesmen who have some underlying vested interest to protect, it has all along been a myth — an exaggeration of the truth.

It has always been more of a myth than reality for one basic reason: *in the overwhelming majority of estates in the United States, no "tax consequence" of any type do generally rise, in the first place.* For example, under the tax law that preceded the Tax Reform Act of 1976 (which had allowed only $60,000 in federal estate tax exemption, plus the marital deduction allowance), the proportion of estates which was subject to federal estate tax was only 7 per cent of all estates. Just 7 per cent! The remaining 93 per cent were not large enough to be taxable; hence no big, extraordinary tax expertise would have really been called for concerning those. Then came the Tax Reform Act of 1976 which, principally by providing a much larger exemption and marital deduction allowance, curtailed the number of estates that were subject to federal estate taxation still further — down to a mere 3 per cent of all estates per year (from the previous 7 per cent)!

But, even then, many lawyers had remained unmoved, and would still pretend that "tax planning" in estate planning in general, and in Will-making, in particular, was of such a crucial importance in the average estate. Then, on August 31, 1981, Congress dropped the other shoe: it passed the ***Economic Recovery Tax Act of 1981.*** By this law, the proportion of all estates that could be subject to Federal transfer taxes was still reduced further—to a tiny 1/3 of 1 per cent of all estates, according to figures provided by Congressional staff members! (Congress did this primarily by dramatically raising the Federal "exemption" ceiling [the size of estate assets that can be transferred to one's heirs tax-free], and by making all property that passes from one spouse to a surviving spouse totally exempt from federal estate taxes—the so-called *"unlimited marital deduction."*)

Translated, what it all boils down to is that, from 1987 (when all the changes of the 1981 law become fully effective), *fewer than 5 estates out of every 1,000 would possibly have been subject to any federal estate taxes, compared to about 28 out of every 1,000 previously. To put it in more relevant, personal terms, what this means for you, the average estate planner or Will-maker, is that for all practical purposes you probably don't have to worry about needing any or fancy special expertise in estate tax*

[1]In a recent article on the subject, for example, a lawyer who would have ordinarily been expected to take a less than conventional lawyers' view, an author of a "do-it-yourself" Will guide and an ardent supporter of the self-help law approach, was cited as holding to the same rather misleading notion that one necessarily needs to use a lawyer if, as the writer put it, "the estate is worth more than $600,000 and therefore likely to be subject to the federal estate tax." (See statement attributed to Denis Clifford in "The Do-It-Yourself Will: Good Idea, Sometimes," N.Y. Times, Sept. 23, 1993 p. 36.)

planning; only if you happen to be so blessed as to belong to that tiny minority of Americans who fall within the society's uppermost wealth brackets may you begin to worry!

The central point is that the claim often voiced by tax lawyers and some estate planning professionals that the average Will-drafter needs some great expertise in estate tax code methods and planning, is a little too overstated. Some knowledge of some basic procedures, maybe. But nothing really extraordinary or critical by any means!

Indeed, in all fairness, many experts, lawyers as well as non-lawyers, have changed their tune, somewhat, and would now admit to the new reality. Said one such expert, John W. Hamm of the New York accounting firm of Arthur Young & Company, "It used to take a lot of maneuvering to try to divvy up an estate appropriately. We would try to utilize both spouses' maximum tax credits and try to take advantage of the progressive estate tax rates by splitting the estate. But both of these areas have changed drastically as a result of the new (1981) law."

"It [the new 1981 law] would, of course, create an enormous change in our perspective towards planning," said another estate plan professional, Sondra Miller, a New York lawyer and member of the Westchester County Estate Planning Council. "[For example] now, if an estate is not going to be taxed until it is in excess of $600,000, much of the old techniques of planning are going to be out the window."[2]

B. LOOK, IS YOUR ESTATE BIG ENOUGH TO BE TAXABLE, IN THE FIRST PLACE?

The point is that, as a factual matter, the 1981 tax law has just about made it absolutely certain that for the overwhelming majority of estates in the United States any exercise in elaborate "tax planning" gimmickry in trust or will-making will now more than ever be neither too fruitful nor necessary. Or, to put it another way, it is for only a very tiny portion of all estates in America — some 1/3 of one percent of the total which fall within the society's uppermost wealth bracket — that an estate taxation "problem" actually exists! Hence, in light of this reality, we elect in this chapter to focus on an aspect of the tax issue which, in the author's view, is even the more primary and relevant tax question for the vast majority of estate plan makers vis-a-vis tax planning, namely: DO YOU HAVE A BIG ENOUGH ESTATE THAT IS TAXABLE, IN THE FIRST PLACE?

Think about it for a moment. If your estate is not big enough and would not be subject to a tax, in the first place, then isn't the issue clearly a mute one for you as to how much of a "tax saving" you could supposedly make by drafting a Will (or a trust) in one way, rather than another, or by having it drawn up by a lawyer as opposed to yourself!?

The Two Types Of Taxes That Are Relevant Here: Estate Taxes And 'Inheritance' or 'Death' Taxes

There are primarily two kinds of taxes to which an estate which qualifies to be taxed may be subject: **1)** Federal estate tax — which is one imposed by the federal government on a decedent's entire "taxable estate"; and **2)** State inheritance tax (also known as state "estate", "inheritance" or "succession" tax) — which is a kind of the right-to-transfer-property tax imposed by most state governments upon that part (and only that part) of the decedent's estate transferred as inheritance to particular beneficiaries. Of the two kinds of taxes, the Federal estate tax is by far the major one to concern yourself with, not only because it is often the much larger one, but also because most states which impose state death or inheritance taxes use the federal tax figures as the "base" from which the state tax is calculated.

Now, back to the main question at hand. The primary question of course, is: what makes an estate subject to an estate tax liability?

The answer is simple. ***Whether an estate will be taxable will be dependent entirely on one major consideration:*** THE SIZE AND NATURE OF THE ESTATE ASSETS. Under the internal Revenue Code of 1981, the federal estate tax return (from which a tax liability, if any, is determined) is not even required to be filed, <u>unless</u> the value of a decedent's "gross estate" approximately exceeds the following amounts as of the date of death:

---

[2]Along the same line, Michael Richards of HALT, the Washington DC. legal reform organization, states bluntly that: "The long-term effect of the new estate tax law will be to reduce taxpayers' dependence on estate lawyers.... As fewer estates become subject to federal tax, the need for retaining an estate lawyer for tax planning will be eliminated."

	No filing unless gross estate
For death in or gifts made in:	Is More than:
1981	$175,000
1982	225,000
1983	275,000
1984	325,000
1985	400,000
1986	500,000
1987 through 1997	600,000
1998	625,000
1999	650,000
2000 and 2001	675,000
2002 and 2003	700,000
2004	850,000
2005	950,000
2006 and after	1,000,000

NOTE: Note that these limits cease to apply if the beneficiary is the giver's spouse. That is, when the gift is between spouses, the tax-free amount that may be transferred is "unlimited," meaning that it would then be any amount whatsoever (see footnote on p. 69 below). Furthermore, if you made any gifts of "taxable" nature to others (i.e., gifts made to others during your lifetime that are over and above the $10,000 per person permitted annually), such gifts — to the extent that they exceed the $10,000 per person allowed — will be used to reduce the amount of your gross estate that can pass tax-free at your death.

To put it simply, therefore, here's the "acid test": if the value of your "gross estate" is not likely to exceed the above amount in the given years, your estate would probably not be a "taxable estate" for federal estate tax purposes! (Another way of saying this is that these amounts represent for the appropriate years, what you can transfer to any one(s) you prefer, free of federal estate tax.) To put it another way, what this means for you, as an estate planner (or Will-maker), is this: if you can't see the size of your "gross estate" being worth in excess of the above-given "maximum exemption" limits (basically, $1,000,000 as from 2006 onwards), then for all practical purposes you shouldn't worry about having any federal estate tax problems or liability. *And, if you determine that you are in that situation, you should just as well skip the rest of this chapter and forget all the big, fancy talks about estate tax 'planning' for your estate!* [3]

C. FIRST, ESTIMATE THE SIZE OF YOUR "GROSS ESTATE"

As explained above, the size of your "gross estate" is a central figure in determining whether or not you may have to file a federal estate tax return, or possibly have a federal estate tax liability. Hence, the all-important question is: how do you determine this figure—THE SIZE OF YOUR GROSS ESTATE?

The Gross Estate

With respect to determining a person's (or decendent's) "gross estate" for tax purposes, technically speaking there is really one (and only one) important thing to bear in mind: namely, that as defined by the IRS the "gross estate" comprises MORE THAN just the property owned outright by the decedent or only intended by him to pass through his Will, and does, also, include different other kinds of property, including even those property

---

[3]One knowledgeable tax practitioner, Julian S. Bush of the New York law firm of Shea & Gould, put it quite accurately this way: "A [married] couple whose assets are not expected to go above a combined $600,000 need not get involved with fancy [tax planning techniques in] Wills. Above that number, it gets more complicated."

which he may not have owned completely or outrightly.[4] Briefly summarized, a decedent's "gross estate" can be defined as ***roughly the total of everything the decedent owned or shared an interest in, or that is due to his estate.***

For our limited purposes in this manual, however, it will suffice for you to simply define your estimated "gross estate" as follows: ESTIMATED "NET WORTH"—that is, your assets minus liabilities. (See chapter 3, especially the Financial Information section of the Estate Information Worksheet on pp. 21-2). This should suffice for the purposes here, since, after all, you really don't need to know the precise value of your gross estate to be able to do the planning work intelligently; you merely need to have, for our purposes here, a rough but educated estimate so that you can assess the likelihood of your being liable for (federal) estate taxes, if at all.

D. NEXT, DETERMINE IF YOUR ESTATE IS A "TAXABLE ESTATE" BY SUBTRACTING FROM IT THE "ALLOWABLE DEDUCTIONS"

Alright. Let's say you have now calculated the value of your gross estate, meaning, actually, the value of your net worth. The next relevant question for you is this: is the estate big enough to be classified as a "taxable estate"?

How do you make this determination of an estate? It's simple: from your "gross estate" (i.e., your net worth) figure, you then subtract the total of all the "allowable deductions" (p. 69). And whatever balance you have left thereafter (if any), is the "taxable estate." If no balance is left, then the estate at issue is a non-taxable estate — one that would owe no federal estate tax whatsoever.

What constitutes the "allowable deductions" of an estate?

---

[4]More specifically, as more fully defined by the IRS (See IRS Publications 559 and 448, for example), one's gross estate would include such items as the following:

i)   All property of any kind owned by the decedent (or testator) at the time of his death, regardless of where it is located, and that was transferred at death by Trust or Will or by local intestacy laws: real property, stocks, bonds, furniture, personal effects, jewelry, works of art, interest in a business, cash surrender value (or installment proceeds) of life insurance on another's life, notes, and other evidences of indebtedness to the decedent, etc.

ii) Gifts made or property transferred for less than full and adequate consideration within 3 years of decedent's death. [Bona fide sales made for adequate consideration, or gifts (other than a life insurance policy) for which the decedent was not required to file a gift tax return, are not includable as part of the decedent gross estate. However, gift taxes paid on any gifts made during this 3-year period is includable.]

iii) Under most circumstances, the proceeds of a life insurance policy, including accidental death policies, even if they are paid directly to the named beneficiary by the insurance company.

iv) The value of any annuities (or other payments) payable to any other person surviving the decedent (to the extent of the contributions made to it by both the decedent and the employer, if payment to the beneficiary is under a "non qualified plan," and by the decedent only, if payment to the beneficiary is made under a "qualified plan.") [The value of any long-term (over 36 months of) annuity payment to a beneficiary — other than an executor — under the Individual Retirement Arrangement (IRA), is generally excluded, however, as part of a decedent's gross estate.]

v)   With respect to all pre-1977 joint interests, the total value of property owned (or held) by the decedent andothers as joint tenants (or as tenants by the entirety) with the right of survivorship — except the part, if any, proven as paid for by the other surviving joint tenant or tenants.

vi) With respect to all "qualified joint interests" (as well as pre-1977 joint interests for which an election is made to treat them as qualified joint interests), only one-half of the fair market value of the joint interests is includable in the gross estate of the spouse who died first, even if the surviving spouse furnished the total purchase money for the property. (The term "qualified joint interest" for an estate of a person dying after 1981 is defined as any interests in property held by the decedent and the decedent's spouse as: 1) tenants by the entirety, or 2) as joint tenants with the right of survivorship, but only if the spouses are the only joint tenants.)

vii) Life insurance proceeds on decedent's life, if it is payable to his estate or to another person for the benefit of his estate; the proceeds of a policy payable to other beneficiaries but over which the decedent had some "incidents of ownership" (meaning things like the right to change the beneficiary, or to cancel, assign or borrow against the policy);

viii) Insurance proceeds on another's life (to the extent of the cash surrender value of the policy);

ix) Any income earned but still uncollected by the decedent at the time of his death;

x)   Property over which the decedent had 'a general power of appointment' (meaning the right to name who the property should go to);

xi) Distributions from pension and profit-sharing plans made in lump-sum to decedent's beneficiaries;

xii) Dower or curtesy (or statutory estate in lieu thereof) of the surviving spouse.

The Allowable Deductions (From the Gross Estate)

In a word, "allowable deductions" are simply the kinds and amounts of deductions the law says are allowable under the tax code as legitimate to be made from the "gross estate" to arrive at one's "taxable estate." (This would seem logical since the taxable estate is defined as the "gross estate," minus the total "allowable deductions," remember?)

Briefly defined, the following are what constitute the 'allowable deductions' of an estate:

i) the total funeral expenses of the decedent;

ii) the total amount of expenses made (or losses suffered) in administering the estate;

iii) the total debts owed by, or claims made against, the estate;

iv) losses in the estate arising from theft or casualties (storms, fires, and the like), incurred during the settlement of the estate — to the extent that is not compensated for by insurance or otherwise;

v) marital deduction allowance[5]—the value of any and all property passing to the surviving spouse through joint ownership, by Will, by being a beneficiary under life insurance upon decedent's death, by gift or in trust for which the principal of the trust passes to the survivor's own estate at her death, or for which the survivor has a "general" (i.e., sole) power to appoint whom the trust principal would go to, or any other property passing by other means, and which "qualifies" for the marital deduction; and

vi) charitable deduction allowance—the value of property or gifts in the decedent's gross estate donated by the decedent either during his lifetime or by Will to charity.

E. COMPUTING THE "NET" FEDERAL TAX LIABILITY OF AN ESTATE

It has been explained above that the "taxable estate" (what is left after you deduct the total "allowable deductions" from the "gross estate"), is the amount upon which the estate tax liability is assessed. Using the tax table, called the ***Unified Federal Estate And Gift Tax Rate Schedule*** (see p. 73), you can easily determine what is known as the "tentative tax" on the taxable estate you have arrived at — the tax which an estate of a given size would likely be liable for.

In using this schedule to compute the tentative tax, however, there's one more factor of great importance to take into account. The law provides for a system of **"credits"** that can be applied, on a straight dollar-for-dollar basis, as offsets against the tentative tax amount — that is, credits that may be used to reduce the tax (the "tentative tax") assessed on one's estate, dollar-for-dollar. A "credit" is a direct reduction of the tax itself, as distinguished from a "deduction." In other words, what this means is that an estate may show a "tentative tax" liability but still not necessarily owe or have to pay any tax, nevertheless. So long as the amount of previously unused "credits" available to the estate (if any), is <u>in excess</u> of the "tentative tax" amount assessed to it, then that estate would have no "net" estate tax payable, and would in effect be a non-taxable estate.

There are five types of **"credits"** allowable against an estate's tentative tax (on the combined total of the taxable estate and the adjusted taxable gifts) to determine the "net estate tax payable": Unified credit (representing credit for lifetime gifts); credit for state death taxes paid; credit for gift taxes paid; credit for tax on prior transfers; and credit for foreign death taxes.

To illustrate the computation method, let's look at some examples just to see how the tax Schedule (see p. 73 below) is read.

---

[5] NOTE THIS: Marital deduction is a deduction allowable to only a surviving spouse from the decedent partner's gross estate, providing the property on which such allowance is made "qualifies." For estates of spouses who die after 1981, this allowance is unlimited — i.e., it could be any amount or proportion of the estate property, even to the extent of the whole estate, and which "qualifies."

Basically, in making the estate tax computation, the way the marital deduction allowance works out is that the total of any property that have gone or will go to the surviving spouse, say the wife, is deducted from the estate of the deceased spouse, and. any property inherited by the surviving spouse as a marital deduction allowance goes untaxed, but is later taxable in her (the surviving spouse's) own estate when she dies. (See pp. 70-2 for more on actual estate tax computation procedures.)

To be eligible for this deduction, the property involved must "qualify"; that is: i) the property must actually be going to or have gone to the surviving spouse; ii) the spouse must survive the decedent and must be legally married at the time of death; iii) the property must have been denoted or bequeathed to her/him under conditions which make the property includable in his/her own taxable estate when he/she dies.

F. SCHEMATIC ILLUSTRATION OF FEDERAL ESTATE TAX COMPUTATION METHOD FOR 4 DIFFERENT ESTATES

EXAMPLE I: Assume the following facts: Mr. A died in 1994. His gross estate was valued at $800,000. He made no lifetime taxable gifts. His surviving spouse was to receive all the assets of the estate.
The estate tax is computed as follows:

Gross Estate (use, essentially, the net worth).........		$800,000
Minus: (allowable deductions) i) Funeral expenses	$20,000	
ii) Administration expenses	40,000	
iii) Estate debts & losses	100,000	
iv) Charitable deductions.........................	40,000	
		-200,000
Adjusted Gross Estate.......................................		600,000
Minus: Marital deduction (Mr. A left everything to spouse)		-600,000
Taxable Estate...		-0-
Add: Adjusted taxable gifts* (assuming none)........................		-0-
Taxable Amount		-0-
NET ESTATE TAX PAYABLE BY MR. A's ESTATE		-0-

Example 2: Assume the following facts: Mr. B estimates that the value of his gross estate (his net worth) today is about $4.9 million. He anticipates the exemptions and allowable deductions and expenses (funeral and administrative expenses, charitable gifts, etc.) will amount to approximately $400,000, as listed in the illustration below, leaving him a Net Estate of about $4,500,000. He plans to leave $3,250,000 to his wife, and $1,250,000 to his children.

Explanation: First, the property ($3,250,000) Mr. B leaves his wife is totally exempt from any federal estate tax because of the "unlimited marital deductions." Mr. B is thus left with a remaining net estate of $1,250,000 which is subject to federal estate tax. Looking at Column C of the Tax Rates Chart (p. 73), you find that the tax assessable on a $1,250,000 estate is $448,300. From this $448,300 Mr. B deducts the amount for "tax credit" allowed every individual, $192,800.* That leaves the balance of $255,500, which represents the estimated federal estate tax that Mr. B's estate will pay.

Gross Estate (use, basically, the net worth).........		$4,900,000
Minus (allowable deductions): i) Funeral expenses	$60,000	
ii) Administration expenses	90,000	
iii) Estate debts & losses	150,000	
iv) Charitable deductions.........................	100,000	
		-400,000
Adjusted Gross Estate.......................................		4,500,000
Minus: Marital deduction..		-3,250,000
Taxable Estate...		1,250,000
Add: Adjusted taxable gifts* (assuming none)........................		-0-
Taxable Amount		1,250,000
Tax assessable on $1,250,000 .... $448,300		
Less "credits": Unified Credits* .... -192,800		
NET ESTATE TAX PAYABLE BY MR. B's ESTATE		$255,500

*See Footnote on p. 72 for definition of this concept.

Example 3: Let's just say that Mr. C has a net taxable estate (that is, what would be left of the estate after all the 'allowable deductions', such as the funeral and administrative expenses, charitable gift exemptions, marital deductions, etc. shall have been deducted), amounting to $1,300,000. But, the individual exemption of $600,000 has not been deducted at this point.

His estate is computed as follows:

Gross Estate.. $1,800,000

Minus:
    i)   Funeral expenses $50,000
    ii) Administration expenses 40,000
    iii) Estate debts & losses 100,000
    iv) Charitable deductions..10,000

    -200,000

Adjusted Gross Estate...1,600,000
Minus: Marital deduction..-300,000
Taxable Estate...1,300,000
Add: Adjusted taxable gifts* (assuming none)..-0-
Taxable Amount 1,300,000

    Tax assessable on $1,300,000 ....$469,800
    Less "credits": Unified Credits*...-192,800
NET ESTATE TAX PAYABLE BY MR. B's ESTATE $277,000

EXPLANATION OF METHOD OF CALCULATION:

1. Enter the numbers in Column A and B between which the value of your Net Taxable Estate falls	Column A = $1,250,000 Column B = $1,500,000
2. Subtract from the value of your net estate the amount in Column A	$1,300,000 -1,250,000 50,000
3. Multiply this remainder by the applicable percentage in Column D.....................................	50,000 X .43 $21,500
4. Add together the resultant amount and the tax for $1,250,000 listed in Column C	21,500 +448,300 469,800
5. Subtract the federal estate tax credit ($192,800) from the last amount.................................	469,800 -192,800
This is your ESTATE TAX PAYABLE————————▶	277,000

EXAMPLE 4: (Illustrating how the "credits" are made use of): Assume the following: In 1979, while still alive, Mr. D gave his daughter a gift of property valued at $253,000, for which he had filed a gift tax return and paid a net gift tax of $32,800 (tentative tax, $70,800, minus unified credit of $38,000). He made no other prior gifts. Mr. D died in 1982 with a gross estate valued at $607,000. State death taxes of $25,000 were paid by the estate. The estate is valued as of the date of death. The value of the gift as of that date was $300,000.

The net estate tax on Mr. D's estate is computed as follows: [The value of the gift to the daughter at date of Mr. D's death — $300,000 — is not included in the gross estate; but the value of the gift taxes paid ($25,000) would be. However, the taxable gift ($250,000)** is added to the taxable estate for purposes of determining the gross estate tax. No marital deduction is applicable.]

---

*See footnote on p. 72 for definition of this concept.

**The permissible limit for non-taxable gifts under the law operating when the gift was made (1979) was $3,000 per recipient (it's now $10,000 as of this writing since 1981). Hence, any gift in excess of the $3,000 limit is a "taxable gift" meaning $253,000—$3,000 or $250,000 in our present example.

Gross Estate $607,000

Minus:
     i)   Funeral expenses $15,000
     ii) Administration expenses.................45,000
     iii) Estate debts & losses......................37,000
     iv) Charitable deductions ....<u>10,000</u>

                                                               -107,000

Taxable Estate...500,000
Add: Adjusted taxable gifts[6] ($253,000-$3,000) ....+<u>250,000</u>
Taxable Amount..<u>.750,00</u>
Tentative Tax (computed on Taxable Amount from the Unified Rate Schedule) 248,300
Minus "Credits":[7] Gift taxes payable........$32,800
                          Unified credit................62,800 (limit for the 1982 year)
                          State death tax credit
                          (based on adj. taxable
                          estate of $440,000)..........<u>-10,000</u>

                                                                -105,600

NET ESTATE TAX PAYABLE BY MR. D's ESTATE ....<u>.142, 700</u>

---

[6]**"Adjusted taxable gifts"** include only the value of the taxable gifts that were made by the testator (or decedent) after 1976 and that are not includable in the testator's gross estate. (The permissible limit for non-taxable gifts under the law operating since 1981 is $10,000 per recipient. Hence, any gift in excess of that amount is a "taxable gift.")

[7]NOTE THIS: This is where the "tax credit" comes from. For every individual, the federal tax law exempts from federal estate tax property worth up to $600,000, no matter who he or she leaves the property to—i.e., you are allowable to transfer that much property free of federal estate tax. But, with the one important qualification: this exemption is reduced by "taxable gifts" if any, that such gifts are larger than $10,000 per person per year. Thus, let's say you give $40,000 to your son in a single year, then $30,000 ($40,000 - $10,000) will be subject to gift tax. However, the gift tax assessed is not paid in the year you make this gift; rather, the total amount of the excess taxable gift is deducted from your $600,000 estate/gift exemption.
    The $600,000 exemption works, however, by means of "tax credits" which in effect, exempts the first $192,800 of tax due in an estate—the equivalent of the payable on $600,000.

    There are five types of "credits" allowable against an estate's tentative tax before the "net" estate tax payable is finally arrived at. These are: 1) unified credit (representing credit for lifetime gifts); 2) credit for state death taxes paid; 3) credit for gift taxes paid; 4) credit for tax on prior transfers; and 5) credit for foreign death taxes. A "credit" is a direct reduction of the tax itself, as distinguished from a "deduction."

    In particular, the **"unified credit"** — which is so-called because it may be used to cover tax-free gifts made before death — is a credit of $192,800 that can be used to reduce the transfer tax (which is different from the income tax) on both taxable gifts and estates. And, if a decedent did not make any taxable gifts at all during his/her lifetime, the totality (100%) of the credit can be used to reduce the tax on his estate at his death. (A "taxable gift" is one that does not fall into any of these categories: gifts made by one spouse to another, annual gifts of $10,000 or less per recipient, or charitable contributions).

    Take, for example, the case of a person who dies any time after 1987, meaning that his "unified credit" is $192,800. What this means, in effect, is that lifetime gifts or the estate of this decedent can escape tax entirely if they, together, total no more than $600,000 —since $192,800 is exactly the "tentative" tax chargeable on an estate of that ($600,000) size. Thus, this decedent could have made a taxable gift of, say, $100,000 and left a $500,000 estate — without becoming subject to any federal transfer tax. That is, a combined gifts and estate worth up to $600,000 will not be subject to any federal estate tax.

G. UNITED FEDERAL ESTATE AND GIFT TAX RATES (SCHEDULE)

The following table, the *Unified Federal Estate and Gift Tax Rates,* gives the federal estate and gift tax rates for estates of people who have died after 1987. As discussed elsewhere in this manual (see, for example, pp. 66-7), these taxes will only begin to apply if and when your taxable estate is worth $600,000 or more. Basically, to calculate the tax owed, here's the process: first determine your taxable estate—your net worth, minus the exempt amounts (funeral expenses, charitable gifts, any amount left to a surviving spouse). Then, check on the Tax Rates chart below for the tax owed on the taxable estate. Finally, subtract from that amount the "tax credit" that is allowed for the amount that would be owed on the first $600,000 (appx. $192,000). (Of course, you'll recall from our previous discussion that if you have given gifts of more than $10,000 per year per person during your life, then this "credit" will have to be reduced by the total excess amount of excess gifts over the limit).

Unified Federal Estate and Gift Tax Rates (Schedule)

Column A If taxable estate is more than	Column B But not more than	Column C Tax owed on amounts in A	Column D Rate of tax on excess over amounts in A
$ 0	$ 10,000	$ 0	18%
10,000	20,000	1,800	20
20,000	40,000	3,800	22
40,000	60,000	8,200	24
60,000	80,000	13,000	26
80,000	100,000	18,200	28
100,000	150,000	23,800	30
150,000	250,000	38,800	32
250,000	500,000	70,800	34
500,000	750,000	155,800	37
750,000	1,000,000	248,300	39
1,000,000	1,250,000	345,800	41
1,250,000	1,500,000	448,300	43
1,500,000	2,000,000	555,800	45
2,000,000	2,500,000	780,800	49
2,500,000	-------------	1,025,800	50

74

FEDERAL ESTATE TAX:
HOW MUCH WILL YOUR ESTATE PAY?

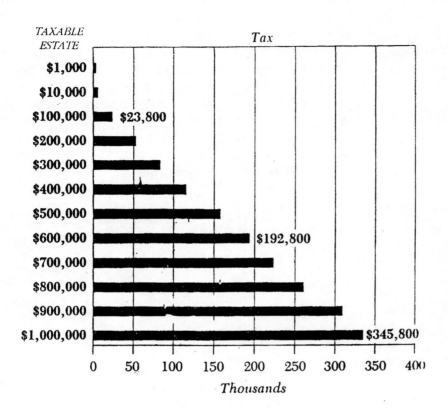

TAXABLE
ESTATE

$1,000	
$10,000	
$100,000	$23,800
$200,000	
$300,000	
$400,000	
$500,000	
$600,000	$192,800
$700,000	
$800,000	
$900,000	
$1,000,000	$345,800

Tax

0   50   100   150   200   250   300   350   4(X)

Thousands

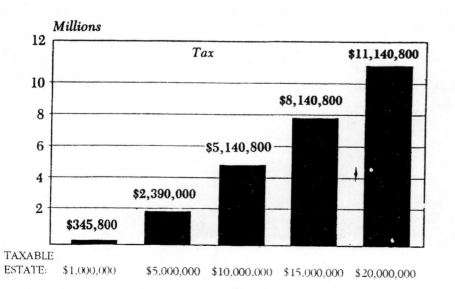

Millions

Tax

$11,140,800

$8,140,800

$5,140,800

$2,390,000

$345,800

TAXABLE
ESTATE: $1,000,000 $5,000,000 $10,000,000 $15,000,000 $20,000,000

Taxing Estates

The Federal marginal tax rate on each portion of a person's estate. No more than 55 percent goes to taxes, but a percent surcharge is imposed on amounts of $10 million to $21.04 million, effectively taxing the entire 55 percent.

60%	$10,000,000
55%	
53%	$3,000,000
49%	$2,500,000
45%	$2,000,000
43%	$1,500,000
41%	$1,250,000
39%	$1,000,000
37%	$ 750,000
TAX-FREE	$ 600,000

Source: Internal Revenue Service

Appendix A
MINIMUM LEGAL REQUIREMENTS FOR A VALID WILL IN EACH OF THE 50 STATES, PUERTO RICO AND DISTRICT OF COLUMBIA

A. Minimum Age Requirements

1. The following states require that the person who makes a Will shall be at least *eighteen (18) years of age:*

Alabama (for personal property only)	Montana
Arizona	Nebraska
Arkansas	Nevada
California	New Hampshire
Colorado	New Mexico
Connecticut	New York
Delaware	North Carolina
Dist. of Columbia (for females only)	North Dakota
Florida	Ohio
Hawaii	Oklahoma
Idaho	Oregon
Illinois	Pennsylvania
Indiana	Rhode Island
Iowa	South Carolina
Kansas	South Dakota
Kentucky	Tennessee
Louisiana	Texas
Maine	Utah
Maryland	Vermont
Massachusetts	Virginia
Michigan	Washington
Minnesota	West Virginia
Mississippi	Wisconsin
Missouri	Wyoming

2. The following states require that the person who makes a Will shall be at least *twenty one (21) years of age:*

Alabama (for real property only)
District of Columbia (for males only)
New Jersey

3. The following states require that the person who makes a Will shall be at least *fourteen (14) years of age:*

Georgia
Puerto Rico

4. The minimum age of *nineteen (19)* is required by only one state, namely the state of Alaska.

B. Required Minimum Mental Condition For A Will-Maker

Each and every state in the Union requires that any person who makes a Will shall be of reasonably sound state of mind *at the time* of his or her making and signing the Will. Briefly, what this means is that the person must have the normal mental (and physical) ability to adequately do or know what he was doing at the time. (A person who, for example, suffers from a condition of insanity or who is underage, or a person who is extremely old or feeble, is suspect.)

C. Minimum Number of Persons Required to Witness a Will

1. The following states require that a testator's Will be witnessed by *at least two (2) persons* of adult age:

Alabama	Montana
Arizona	Nebraska
Arkansas	Nevada
California	New Mexico
Colorado	New York
Connecticut	North Carolina
Delaware	North Dakota
District of Columbia	Ohio
Florida	Oklahoma
Hawaii	Oregon
Idaho	Pennsylvania
Illinois	Rhode Island
Indiana	South Dakota
Iowa	Tennessee
Kansas	Texas
Kentucky	Utah
Maryland	Virginia
Massachusetts	Washington
Michigan	West Virginia
Minnesota	Wisconsin
Mississippi	Wyoming
Missouri	

2. The following states require that the Will be witnessed by *at least three (3) persons* of adult age:

Louisiana	Puerto Rico
Maine	South Carolina
New Hampshire	Vermont

D. Type Of Persons Who Can Be A Witness To Your Will

Lunatics or insane persons are not expressly disqualified from serving as witnesses, except in Alabama; persons convicted of serious crimes are not disqualified to serve as witnesses, except in Alabama; and the deaf, dumb, or the blind are not disqualified to serve as witnesses, except in Louisiana. However, because of the extreme importance of this, it's advisable that you pick as your witnesses persons who are unquestionably of sufficient mental capacity to understand and appreciate the nature of the event they are called upon to witness, and can clearly describe or recount the event if they were to be called upon to do so.

Persons named in a Will as beneficiaries, guardians, trustees, executors or executrixes, are not disqualified to serve as witnesses in any state of the Union. However, there are various restrictions and limitations placed in many states on the amount or kind of gifts such persons may receive under the Will. Thus, in many states,[1] while a Will itself remains legally valid when a beneficiary acts as a witness, the gift made to such a beneficiary under the Will is often void (made invalid), in part or in whole. In any event, just on the face of it, witnesses who are beneficiaries under the Will are liable to look compromised or suspicious, even if not actually incompetent as witnesses.

CAUTION: *To avoid any possible complications in the future, you had better stayed completely away from using a beneficiary as a witness. Use other persons.* One more thing, if you can find MORE witnesses than your state specifically requires in the law, (Section C above), it wouldn't hurt to use more. One (or more) of your witnesses may die; or you may move to a state which requires more witnesses than your present state, or buy property there. This way, you can always be sure that your Will would always remain current and sufficient under any state's rules, no matter where you live or move to (or where the will may turn out being probated).

E. States Which Require a Notary Public to Sign the Will

There's a common belief among many people that to be valid, the testator's signature on the Will itself, is required to be notarized by a Notary Public, or an officer of the court or some other similar official who administers oath. Actually, this belief is mistaken. There is, in fact, only one state with that requirement — Louisiana. The Louisiana law requires three witnesses to a Will itself, one of whom should be a Notary Public licensed to acknowledge signatures.

[NOTE: Note that, on the other hand, the signatures of the witnesses to the Will, as differentiated from the testator himself, may be notarized, but this will usually be on a separate sheet of paper that is then attached to the Will — See Self-Proving *Affidavit Of Subscribing or Attesting Witnesses* on p. 36].

F. States Which Permit Holographic (Or Olographic) Wills

Holographic Wills (Section I of Chapter 2, at p. 14) are expressly authorized in the following states:[2]

Alaska	New York
Arizona	North Carolina
Arkansas	North Dakota
California	Oklahoma
Colorado	South Dakota
Idaho	Tennessee
Louisiana	Texas
Maryland	Utah
Mississippi	Virginia
Montana	West Virginia
Nebraska	Wyoming
Nevada	

[1] These states include: Arkansas, Connecticut, District of Columbia, Hawaii, Idaho, Illinois, Indiana, Iowa, Kansas, Kentucky, Maine, Maryland, Michigan, Mississippi, Missouri, Nevada, New Hampshire, and Texas.

[2] Note that various states generally specify special requirements and conditions under which Holographic and Noncupative Wills shall become acceptable in lieu of the Regular Will — who may make them, the type of property or limits thereof which may be given away by them, the number of witnesses needed, under what conditions they may be made, etc.

G. States Which Permit Nuncupative Wills

Nuncupative (i.e., oral) Wills (see Section I of Chapter 2, at p. 14) are expressly authorized as valid in the following states:[3]

Alabama	New York
Alaska	North Carolina
California	North Dakota
District of Columbia	Oklahoma
Indiana	South Dakota
Kansas	Tennessee
Louisiana	Texas
Maine	Utah
Massachusetts	Virginia
Michigan	West Virginia
Mississippi	Wyoming
Missouri	

H. States Which Permit Wills to be Revoked by Making a Codicil or a New Will

Without exception, an existing Will can be validly revoked or cancelled in every state by either one of these two methods: **i)** by tearing up the old Will and (promptly) making a new one which contains a statement to the effect that you revoke all previous Wills and codicils; or **ii)** by properly making out a Codicil (an amendment) to the old Will, with a statement in the codicil expressly revoking the old Will or some similar or specific provisions therein to that effect. (See Chapter 5, Section B at pp. 39-40 for more on the amendment and revocation of a Will).

---

[3]See footnote #2 on p. 77.

Appendix B

A SEPARATE LETTER OR MEMO OF INSTRUCTIONS & INFORMATION YOU SHOULD LEAVE ALONGSIDE YOUR WILL (AN ILLUSTRATIVE SAMPLE)

The following is a rather excellent but actual letter and memo of instructions left by a New York testator (a non-lawyer) for his Executor to assist his executor in better discharging his duties under the Will. The actual name of the testator, since deceased in 1992, and all identifying information relative to the estate, have been intentionally altered by the writer so as to protect the decedent's privacy. The letter is illustrative only, meant simply to give an idea of what a good letter or memo of this sort should typically look like or cover.

LETTER OF INSTRUCTIONS & INFORMATION TO AID IN THE DISTRIBUTION AND SETTLEMENT OF THE ESTATE AND AFFAIRS OF MR. FALA MERCED COLO, A/K/A MERCED COLO

Personal Information

Bank accounts at American Savings Bank, 111th St., & Broadway (Manhattan, N.Y.)

Savings:	*#032013242 8*
	#0321568926 (Ready Investment)
Checking:	*#032840936 4*

IRA's and CD's

IRA: *#0356785304*
        Balance $2,612.26   *Maturity: 1/3/92*
        Effective: 6/3/89   *Interest Rate: 8.15%*

IRA   *#0356834383*
        Balance: $1,210.55   *Maturity: 12/21/91*
        Effective: 10/20/89   *Interest Rate: 7.23%*

IRA   *#0356759317*
        Balance: $1,363.84   *Maturity: 10/7/91*
        Effective: 10/7/89   *Interest Rate: 7.65%*

CD   *#0321629884*
        Balance: $1,244.78   *Maturity: 11/20/91*
        Effective: 3/31/90   *Interest Rate: 7.97%*

CD   *#032162876*
        Balance: $2,937.41   *Maturity: 1/3/92*
        Effective: 9/30/90   *Interest Rate: 8.16%*

CD   *#0321644545*
           Balance: $2,933.38   Maturity: 7/5/91
           Effective: 9/30/90   Interest Rate: 6.63%

My Social Security Number: *101-16-6979*
My Medicare Number: *101-16-5979A*

AARP Membership: *#65629736 (Cards in my wallet)*

Safety Deposit Box at ASB—#1163. Key #1085 in my purse.

*Postal Box at Cathedral Station, 104th St., NYC 10025 - #735
   in the name of FMC Publications/Merced Colo.*

Charge Accounts—*Department Stores*
Lord & Taylor, #202-858-34   Macy's, #795-28-636
Saks Fifth Avenue, #19-516-971   Bloomingdale's, #175-11-503
Bergdorf Goodman, #206-325-327

Credit Cards: *Citibank #5424-1800-1790-2113 (Mastercard)*

Trivia: *1. Tax Forms on top shelf of hall closet across from my bedroom.
   2. Don't notify Columbia Un. [University, the landlord]. Continue to pay rent and bills in my name until Will is settled and everything distributed.
   3. Probate kit to Probate a Will without lawyer, you can get at 24 Commerce St., Suite 1732, [Do-It-Yourself Legal Publishers], ($75).*

Stock Certificates in Safe Deposit Box

Name of Stock	No. of Shares	Certificate No.
Acme Steel Co.	15	
Interlake Iron	10 dated 09/09/55	C0104354
Interlake Corporation	15 dated 11/24/86	IK34922
Interlake Inc.	05 dated 09/11/75	C049858
Pacific Gas & Electric	57 dated 06/15/83	ZQ S70726
" " "	03 dated 03/21/73	CJ 26626
" " "	10 dated 05/05/54	NF 571587
" " "	02 dated 07/20/70	SNF 0321450
" " "	02 dated 07/02/64	SNF 150274
" " "	01 dated 06/22/56	NF 612284
" " "	01 dated 07/05/61	NF 766265
" " "	01 dated 07/08/58	NF 682903
" " "	05 dated 10/15/74	CJ 91381
" " "	06 dated 05/20/75	CJ 226138
" " "	26 dated 01/19/62	J 26058
	114 shares	

*Wilson Organic Chemicals, Inc, 50 Shares 07/16/54
   Corporate Seal 1947 NJ
(These could be worthless). Check it. Schwab [stock brokers] has nothing on it.*

INSTRUCTIONS FOR SETTLING MY PERSONAL AFFAIRS (cont'd)

I do not have life insurance. Funeral expenses to be paid from estate.

<u>*Notify*</u>*: Social Security Administration*
    <u>*Tel*</u>*: 1-800-234-5772   (I think they give money for burial.)*
    AARP - I pay monthly
    <u>*Tel*</u>*: 1 800-523-5800*

    ALLSTATE INSURANCE— to cancel insurance on my apartment at the proper time.
    Policy #O-03-730l119 02/11
    Agent: Rob A. Towns   <u>Tel:</u> (212) 695-7265

<u>*Distribution of Property*</u>

In the "typewriter & exercycle room," in the second drawer of the broken chest of drawers, there is a box on the left that contains important papers. Among these in an envelope are the deeds to cemetery plots. I have discontinued paying for the Linden Hill plot where my mother and grandparents were buried. The yearly amount was paid since my mother died in 1945. That's enough. I checked with them a couple of years ago and the plot will just remain as is.

Deed to Bide-a-Wee Animal Cemetery, where Perrie is buried There's room for one more burial. Perrie was buried in a casket, but my three Persians will be cremated.

<u>*My Pets*</u>

One of the most important things on my mind is the welfare of my three Persian cats Nikki, Polly and Mitzi, whom I love dearly. I have given this very careful thought.

There is no such thing as getting them a good home. They've had the best and have received a great amount of love and attention all their lives. The surroundings would be strange and they do not take to strangers or animals. Also, there is the matter of their ages. On October 16/91 Nikki will be 15. On December 20, 1991, Polly will be 13, and on September 12, Mitzi will be 11. Through my special care I've been able to keep them in perfect health. Therefore, the best solution is that they be put to sleep and cremated. All 3 urns can be buried in the Bide-a-Wee plot where Perrie is buried.

Since you probably don't know anything about this, Sheila Katz can help. It is a simple injection for each.

The Parakeets go to my cousin, William Otero, since they are also his. He should get my books on parakeets so that he'll know how to keep them healthy.

<u>*Furniture*</u>

My bedroom furniture was expensive. It's Heritage. Living room furniture (loveseats) was also expensive. Maybe someone might want to buy. If not, I guess they'll have to be given away to the beneficiaries who might want them. You decide. Other furniture can be given to the Salvation Army or one of those organizations, or just throw out.

<u>*Piano*</u>

Should be offered to my grandmother's church in the Bronx—Iglesia Luterana_____on_____

Avenue.   Tell them it was my grandmother's church for many years when Rev._____ was pastor. Maybe the church can get someone to move it free, or cheaply. If it's not too expensive, and they can't get someone to move it, the Estate could pay for it. A latin mover (hopefully religious) perhaps in the Bronx, might be cheaper.

If they don't want it, in the Yellow Pages there are dealers who buy vintage pianos. Mine used to be a pianola and is a Raymond by the Jansen Piano Co. who were big in the 20's. Since it's no longer a pianola, it probably won't bring in too much money, although it could be restored to pianola since they do great restoration jobs.

VCR

If you want it, Frank, you may have it, but I want Bill Otero to get some of the tapes. Let him choose the ones he wants.

TV's

The 2-inch Bronsonic in my bedroom goes to Bill Otero since he paid for the repairs the time he dropped it. The Weltron, which needs repairs since it's not working, is quite expensive and excellent, with 8 track tapes. This was given to me by a millionaire I worked for who bought only expensive things. Whoever is willing to have it repaired, may have it. Whoever wants the others, may have them.

Artists Material, Easel, Art Books

These go to Matere. Chickie can take care of this.

Booklets "How To Attract Money With Metavision"

Anybody who wants one, may have it. Bank account is closed. If any orders should come in, either return or fill. Deposit in my account at ASB bv proper notation on back such as "Pay to the order of Merced Colo" and stamped with company stamp. Post Office box lease expires in July. They notify. Cancel or keep box for rest of year.

Crochet Bedspreads

One in my bedroom; the other in the trunk. Both for double bed were handmade by my mother and are worth a lot of money. If possible, I would like them sent to Carlos & Isabel in Spain.   If not, then they go to Eli Boss.

Books

What you think best.

Furs & Clothes

My wardrobe goes to my cousin, Alma Gladiar in Canada. You would have to call her on the phone for quick-ness and how to get to her. Anything she doesn't want can go to any of the following: Social Services at St. John's the Divine. It's across from where the booths with guards are, on right driveway of Cathedral. The Salvation Army, Goodwill Industries, Planned Parenthood. Or whatever Alma may decide.

Other household things — plates, cutlery, silverware, pots, pans, to whoever wants them.

Photographic Equipment

(Including cameras, enlarger, etc.) Can be sold second-hand. I leave to your discretion.

Typewriters

One of them is a real antique—goes back to late 20's. There are people who are interested in these things. The electric Smith Corona to whoever wants it.

Anything I've missed I leave to your discretion. You can give to anybody or any organization you want to, or throw out, depending on what it is and its condition.

JEWELRY

Mari Monk— gets my high school ring which is gold and onyx, has a W on the black stone, and 1940 on the sides. She also gets the gold high school key with a W on black stone. My initials are on both of these. (These are among jewelry behind green skirt in my bedroom.) She also gets my animal pins and the black onyx elephant on gold chain. Also, the round Sterling Silver bracelet with flower designs. Silver flower pin with one pearl.

BENEFICIARIES & INSTITUTIONS MENTIONED [IN THE WILL]

1. *First Church Of Religion*   *(Dr. Stu Gray)*
   14 East 50th Street   *Tel: 688-0610*
   New York, New York 10017

2. *American Savings Bank*   *Tel: 749-4600*
   111th Street & Broadway Branch
   New York, New York 10025

3. *William Otero [Executor for Will]*   *Service Department, Evening Staff*
   Sullivan & Cromwell   *Tel: 558-4000*
   128 Broad Street
   New York, New York

4. *The Humane Education Committee*   *Sheila Katz*
   PO Box 445   *Tel: 410-3098*
   New York, New York 10028

5. *Mrs. Mari Monk*   *Tel: (718) 352-2011*
   28-33 Jordan Street
   Flushing, New York 11358

6. *Carlos & Isabel Dominici*   *011-34-6-5848150*
   114 Sierra de Altea
   Altea (Aligante) Spain

7. *Ministry of Prayer*   *When sending them the amount, it*
   United Church of Religious Science   *should go by Certified Mail to be sure it*
   3251 West Sixth Street   *will get to them.*
   PO Box 75127
   Los Angeles, CA 90075-0127

8. *Silent Unity*   *Certified Mail*
   Unity School Of Christianity   *Tel: (816) 524-3551*
   Unity Village, MO 64065

9. *Mrs. Eli Boss [Witness to Will]*   *Tel: (718) 274-0652*
   28-22 49th Street
   Astoria, Queens 11103

10. *Mrs. Alma Gladiar*
    3005 Grenada Road
    Houston, B.C. Canada VOJIZO

11. *Matere Rod [Alternate Executor]*   *Tel: (614) 845-7784*
    2106 Honeywell Avenue
    Bronx, New York

12. *Animal Rights Mobilization*
    503 Broadway, Room 512
    New York, New York

13. *Frank Cord*
    PO Box 1769
    Homestead, Florida 33093

Appendix C

STATUTORY [OR OTHER] LIVING WILL FORMS
FOR ALL 50 STATES

A. States Which Allow Another Person To Sign The Living Will On Behalf Of The Living Will-Maker

The following 25 states specifically allow someone other than the declarant to sign the "Declaration" (the Living Will) for the "Declarant" (the Living Will-maker), if the declarant is unable to do so himself:

Alabama, Alaska, Arkansas, Colorado, Delaware, District of Columbia, Florida, Hawaii, Indiana, Iowa, Kansas, Louisiana, Maine, Maryland, Minnesota, Missouri, Montana, Nevada, New Jersey, North Dakota, South Dakota, Utah, West Virginia, Wisconsin, Wyoming.

B. States Where The State's Specific Statutory Form Is Mandatory

As of this writing and last research, the following 17 states and the District of Columbia expressly require that the "Statutory" Living Will form (the specific form provided under the state's statutes) <u>MUST</u> be precisely or substantially used:

California	Mississippi
District of Columbia*	North Carolina
Georgia	North Dakota*
Idaho	Oklahoma*
Indiana*	Oregon
Kansas*	South Carolina
Kentucky*	Utah
Maryland*	Washington*
Minnesota	Wisconsin

*In these states the law permits that the Living Will-Maker may include additional directives but as long as it's consistent with the suggested form.

This means, in effect, that for the overwhelming balance of the states — that is, in the other 33 states besides the above-listed — you are permitted to draft and use your own individually tailored Living Will, one which presumably is as legally adequate as, or perhaps, even better-drafted than a pre-provided statutory form. In light of that, in the state-by-state listing in the rest of this chapter below, we have opted to list the "statutory" Living Will forms for only those above-listed 18 jurisdictions where it is legally required that ONLY the state-provided form be used. But, for the other 33 states where it is not mandatory that either the statutory or a specific form be used, we have provided for the use and benefit of our readership, a Living Will Declaration form that is more comprehensive than the typical short form prevalent with the state-prescribed forms—*the Publisher's Comprehensive 'General Purpose' LIVING WILL DECLARATION* form set forth on pp. 51-3.

C. Alphabetical Listing Of The State-Prescribed Living Will Form For Each State Where Only Statutory Form Must Be Used

Alabama: Recommended sample Living Will form is on pp. 51-3.

Alaska: Recommended sample Living Will form is on pp.51-3.

Arizona: Recommended sample Living Will form is on pp. 51-3.

Arkansas: Recommended sample Living Will form is on pp. 51-3.

California
Directive to Physicians

Directive made this _____ day of _____ *(month, year).*

I, _____ of _____, fully and voluntarily make known my desire that my life shall not be artificially prolonged under the circumstances set forth below, and do hereby declare:

1. If at any time I should have an incurable injury, disease, or illness certified to be terminal by two physicians, and where the application of life-sustaining procedures would serve only to artificially prolong the moment of my death and where my physician determines that my death is imminent whether or not life-sustaining procedures are utilized, I direct that such procedures be withheld or withdrawn, and that I be permitted to die naturally.

2. In the absence of my ability to give directions regarding the use of such life-sustaining procedures, it is my intention that this directive shall be honored by my family and physician(s) as the final expression of my legal right to refuse medical or surgical treatment and accept the consequences from such refusal.

3. If I have been diagnosed as pregnant and that diagnosis is known to my physician, this directive shall have no force or effect during the course of my pregnancy.

4. 1 have been diagnosed at least 14 days ago as having a terminal condition by_____, M.D., whose address is _____, and whose telephone number is _____. I understand that if I have not filled in the physician's name and address, it shall be presumed that I did not have a terminal condition when I made out this directive.

5. This directive shall have no force or effect five years from the date filled in above.

6. I understand the full import of this directive and I am emotionally and mentally competent to make this directive.

Signed, ✗ _____
(signature)
City, County and State of Residence _____

The declarant has been personally known to me and I believe him or her to be of sound mind.

Witness ✗ _____
(name & signature)
Witness ✗ _____
(name & signature)

Colorado: Recommended sample Living Will form is on pp. 51-3.

Connecticut: Recommended sample Living Will form is on pp. 51-3.

District Of Columbia
Declaration

Declaration made this_____ day of _____ *(month, year)*.

I, _____, being of sound mind, willfully and voluntarily make known my desires that my dying shall not be artificially prolonged under the circumstances set forth below, and do declare:

If at any time I should have an incurable injury, disease or illness certified to be a terminal condition by two (2) physicians who have personally examined me, one (1) of whom shall be my attending physician, and the physicians have determined that my death will occur whether or not life-sustaining procedures are utilized, and where the application of life-sustaining procedures would serve only to artificially prolong the dying process, I direct that such procedures be withheld or withdrawn, and that I be permitted to die naturally with only the administration of medication or the performance of any medical procedure deemed necessary to provide me with comfort care or to alleviate pain.

Other directions:_____
_____
_____
_____
_____
_____

In the absence of my ability to give directions regarding the use of such life-sustaining procedures, it is my intention that this declaration shall be honored by my family and physician(s) as the final expression of my legal right to refuse medical or surgical treatment and accept the consequences from such refusal.

I understand the full import of this declaration and am emotionally and mentally competent to make this declaration.

Signed ✗ _____
(Declarant's signature)
Address _____

I believe the declarant to be of sound mind. I did not sign the declarant's signature above for or at the direction of the declarant. I am at least eighteen (18) years of age and am not related to the declarant by blood or marriage, I am not entitled to any portion of the estate of the declarant according to the laws of intestate succession of the District of Columbia or under any will of declarant or codicil thereto, or directly financially responsible for declarant's medical care. I am not the declarant's attending physician, an employee of the attending physician, or an employee of the health facility in which the declarant is a patient.

Witness ✗ _____
(name & signature)
Witness ✗ _____
(name & signature)

Delaware: Recommended sample Living Will form is on pp. 51-3.

Florida: Recommended sample Living Will form is on pp. 51-3.

Georgia
Living Will

LIVING WILL MADE THIS _____ DAY OF _____, 19_____.

I, _____, being of sound mind, willfully and voluntarily make known my desire that my life shall not be prolonged under the circumstances set forth below, and do declare:

1. If at any time I should have a terminal condition as defined in and established in accordance with the procedures set forth in paragraph (10) of Code Section 31-32-2 of the Official Code of Georgia Annotated, I direct that the application of life-sustaining procedures to my body be withheld or withdrawn and that I be permitted to die;

2. In the absence of my ability to give directions regarding the use of such life-sustaining procedures, it is my intention that this living will shall be honored by my family and physician(s) as the final expression of my legal right to refuse medical or surgical treatment and accept the consequences of such refusal;

Other instructions: _____

_____

_____

_____

_____

3. 1 understand that I may revoke this living will at any time;

4. 1 understand the full import of this living will, and I am at least 18 years of age and am emotionally and mentally competent to make this living will; and

5. If I am female and I have been diagnosed as pregnant, this living will shall have no force and effect during the course of my pregnancy.

Signed ✗ _____
                          (Will-Maker)

City, County and State of Residence _____

I hereby witness this living will and attest that:

(1) The declarant is personally known to me and I believe the declarant to be at least 18 years of age and of sound mind;

(2) I am at least 18 years of age;

(3) To the best of my knowledge, at the time of the execution of this living will, I:

  (A) Am not related to the declarant by blood or marriage;

  (B) Would not be entitled to any portion of the declarant's estate by any will or operation of law under the rules of descent and distribution of this state;

  (C) Am not the attending physician of the declarant or any employee of the attending physician or an employee of the hospital or skilled nursing facility in which declarant is a patient;

  (D) Am not directly responsible for the declarant's medical care; and

  (E) Have no present claim against any portion of the estate of the declarant;

(4) Declarant has signed this document in my presence as above-instructed, on the date above first shown.

Witness ✗ _____
                          (print & sign name)

Witness ✗ _____

(print & sign name)

Additional witness required when living Will is signed in a hospital or skilled nursing facility.

I hereby witness this living Will and attest that I believe the declarant to be of sound mind and to have made this Living Will willingly and voluntarily.

Witness ✗ _____

(Medical Director of skilled nursing facility or staff physician in the care of the patient, or chief of the hospital medical staff, or staff physician not participating in the care of the patient.)

Hawaii: Recommended sample Living Will form is on pp. 51-3.

Idaho
A Living Will

A Directive to Withhold or Provide Treatment

Directive made this_____ day _____(month, year).

I, _____, being of sound mind, willfully and voluntarily make known my desire that my life shall not be artificially prolonged under the circumstances below, and do hereby declare that:

1. If at any time I should have an incurable injury, disease, illness or condition certified to be terminal by two medical doctors who have examined me, and where the application of life-sustaining procedures of any kind would serve only to prolong artificially the moment of my death, and where a medical doctor determines that my death is imminent, whether or not life-sustaining procedures are utilized, or I have been diagnosed as being in a persistent-vegetative state, I direct that the following marked expression of my intent be followed and that I be permitted to die naturally, and that I receive any medical treatment or care that may be required to keep me free of pain or distress.

Check One Box

☐ If at any time I should become unable to communicate my instructions, then I direct that all medical treatment, care, and nutrition and hydration necessary to restore my health, sustain my life, and to abolish or alleviate pain or distress be provided to me. Nutrition and hydration shall not be withheld or withdrawn from me if I would die from malnutrition or dehydration rather than from my injury, disease, illness or condition.

☐ If at any time I should become unable to communicate my instructions and where the application of artificial life-sustaining procedures shall serve only to prolong artificially the moment of my death, I direct that such procedures be withheld or withdrawn except for the administration of nutrition and hydration.

☐ If at any time I should become unable to communicate my instructions and where the application of artificial life-sustaining procedures shall serve only to prolong artificially the moment of my death, I direct that such procedures be withheld or withdrawn including withdrawal of the administration of nutrition and hydration.

2. In the absence of my ability to give directions regarding the use of life-sustaining procedures, I hereby appoint _____ *(name)* currently residing at_____ as my attorney-in-fact/proxy for making health care decisions in my place; and it is my intention that this appointment shall be honored by him/her, by my family, relatives, friends, physicians and lawyer as the final expression of my legal right to refuse medical or surgical treatment, and I accept the consequences of such a decision. I have duly executed a Durable Power of Attorney for health care decisions on this date.

3. In the absence of my ability to give further directions regarding my treatment, including life-sustaining procedures, it is my intention that this directive shall be honored by my family and physicians as the final expression of my legal right to refuse or accept medical and surgical treatment, and I accept the consequences of such refusal.

4. If I have been diagnosed as pregnant and that diagnosis is known to any interested person, this directive shall have no force during the course of my pregnancy.

5. I understand the full importance of this directive and am emotionally and mentally competent to make this directive. No participant in the making of this directive or in its being carried into effect, whether it be a medical doctor, my spouse, a relative, friend or any other person, shall be held responsible in any way, legally, professionally, or socially, for complying with my directive.

Signed ✗ _____
(Declarant)
City, County and State of residence _____

The declarant has been known to me personally and I believe him/her to be of sound mind.

Witness ✗ _____
(name & signature)
Address_____

Witness ✗ _____
(name & signature)
Address _____

Illinois: Recommended sample Living Will form is on pp. 51-3.

Indiana
Living Will Declaration

Declaration made this_____ day_____ *(month, year).*

I, _____, being at least eighteen (18) years old and of sound mind, willfully and voluntarily make known my desires that my dying shall not be artificially prolonged under the circumstances set forth below, and I declare:

If at any time I have an incurable injury, disease or illness certified in writing to be a terminal condition by my attending physician, and my attending physician has determined that my death will occur within a short period of time, and the use of life-prolonging procedures would serve only to artificially prolong the dying process, I direct that such procedures be withheld or withdrawn, and that I be permitted to die naturally with only the provision of appropriate nutrition and hydration and the administration of medication and the performance of any medical procedure necessary to provide me with comfort care or to alleviate pain.

In the absence of my ability to give directions regarding the use of life-prolonging procedures, it is my intention that this declaration be honored by my family and physician as the final expression of my legal right to refuse medical or surgical treatment and accept the consequences of the refusal.

I understand the full import of this declaration.

Signed ✗ _____
(Declarant)

City, County and State of residence_____

    The declarant has been personally known to me, and I believe (him/her) to be of sound mind. I did not sign the declarant's signature for or at the direction of the declarant. I am not a parent, spouse or child of the declarant. I am not entitled to any part of the declarant's estate or directly financially responsible for the declarant's medical care. I am competent and at least eighteen (18) years old.

Witness ✗_____   Date _____
         (print & sign name)
Witness ✗_____   Date _____
         (print & sign name)

        Iowa: Recommended sample Living Will form is on pp. 51-3.

Kansas
Declaration

      Declaration made this _____day _____*(month, year)*.

I,_____being of sound mind, willfully and voluntarily make known my desires that my dying shall not be artificially prolonged under the circumstances set forth below, and do hereby declare:

    If at any time I should have an incurable injury, disease or illness certified to be a terminal condition by two physicians who have personally examined me, one of whom shall be my attending physician, and the physicians have determined that my death will occur whether or not life-sustaining procedures are utilized and where the application of life-sustaining procedures would serve only to artificially prolong the dying process, I direct that such procedures be withheld or withdrawn, and that I be permitted to die naturally with only the administration of medication or the performance of any medical procedure deemed necessary to provide me with comfort care.

    In the absence of my ability to give directions regarding the use of such life-sustaining procedures, it is my intention that this declaration shall be honored by my family and physician(s) as the final expression of my legal right to refuse medical or surgical treatment and accept the consequences from such refusal.

    I understand the full import of this declaration and I am emotionally and mentally competent to make this declaration.

    Other Directions:_____

_____
_____
_____
_____

Signed ✗ _____
                (Declarant)

City, County and State of Residence _____

The declarant has been personally known to me and I believe him or her to be of sound mind. I did not sign the declarant's signature above for or at the direction of the declarant. I am not related to the declarant by blood or marriage, or entitled to any portion of the estate of the declarant according to the laws of intestate succession or under any will of declarant or codicil thereto, or directly financially responsible for the declarant's medical care.

Witness ✗ _____
(print & sign name)

Witness ✗ _____
(print & sign name)

Kentucky
Declaration

Declaration made this_____day of _____*(month, year).*

I, _____, willfully and voluntarily make known my desire that my dying shall not be artificially prolonged under the circumstances set forth below, and do hereby declare:

If at any time I should have a terminal condition and my attending and one (1) other physician, in their discretion, have determined such condition is incurable and irreversible and will result in death within a relatively short time, and where the application of life-prolonging treatment would serve only to artificially prolong the dying process, I direct that such treatment be withheld or withdrawn, and that I be permitted to die naturally with only the administration of medication or the performance of any medical treatment deemed necessary to alleviate pain or for nutrition or hydration.

Other instructions: _____

_____

_____

_____

In the absence of my ability to give directions regarding the use of such life-prolonging treatment, it is my intention that this declaration shall be honored by my attending physician and my family as the final expression of my legal right to refuse medical or surgical treatment, and I accept the consequences of such refusal.

If I have been diagnosed as pregnant and that diagnosis is known to my attending physician, this directive shall have no force or effect during the course of my pregnancy.

I understand the full import of this declaration and I am emotionally and mentally competent to make this declaration.

STATE OF KENTUCKY)
) Sct.
COUNTY OF   )

Before me, the undersigned authority, on this day personally appeared _____, the Living Will Declarant, and _____ and _____, known to me to be witnesses whose names are each signed to the foregoing instrument, and all these persons being first duly sworn, Mr/Mrs_____, the Living Will Declarant, declared to me and to the witnesses in my presence that the instrument is the Living Will Declaration of the Declarant and that the Declarant has willingly signed, and that such Declarant executed it as a free and voluntary act for the purposes therein expressed; and each of the witnesses stated to me, in the presence and hearing of the Living Will Declarant, that the declarant signed the Declaration as witness and to the best of such witness' knowledge, the Living Will Declarant was eighteen (18) years of age or over, of sound mind and under no constraint or undue influence.

Living Will Declarant: ✗_____

Witness: ✗_____

Address: _____

Witness: ✗_____

Address: _____

SUBSCRIBED, SWORN TO AND ACKNOWLEDGED before me by _____, the Living Will Declarant, and subscribed and sworn to before me by _____ and _____, the witnesses, on this the _____ day of _____ 19____.

     Notary Public State at Large of _____

     Date my Commission expires _____

     Louisiana: Recommended sample Living Will form is on pp. 51-3.

     Maine: Recommended sample Living Will form is on pp. 51-3.

Maryland
Declaration

    If at any time I should have an incurable injury, disease, or illness certified to be a terminal condition by two (2) physicians who have personally examined me, one (1) of whom shall be my attending physician, and the physicians have determined that my death is imminent and will occur whether or not life-sustaining procedures are utilized and where the application of such procedures would serve only to artificially prolong the dying process, I direct that such procedures be withheld or withdrawn, and that I be permitted to die naturally with only the administration of medication, the administration of food and water, and the performance of any medical procedure that is necessary to provide comfort care or alleviate pain. In the absence of my ability to give directions regarding the use of such life-sustaining procedures, it is my intention that this declaration shall be honored by my family and physician(s) as the final expression of my right to control my medical care and treatment.

       Declaration made this_____ day _____ *(month, year)*.

I, _____, being of sound mind, willfully and voluntarily direct that my dying shall not be artificially prolonged under the circumstances set forth in this declaration.

    I am legally competent to make this declaration, and I understand its full import.

Signed ✗ _____
                      (Declarant)

Address _____

Under penalty of perjury, we state that this declaration was signed by _____, in the presence of the undersigned who, at _____ request, in _____ presence, and in the presence of each other, have hereunto signed our names and witness this _____ day of _____ 19___, and declare: The declarant is personally known to me, and I believe the declarant to be of sound mind. I did not sign the declarant's signature to this declaration. Based upon information and belief, I am not related to the declarant by blood or marriage, [or] a creditor of the declarant, [or] entitled to any portion of the estate of the declarant under any existing testamentary instrument of the declarant, [or] entitled to any financial benefit by reason of the death of the declarant, [or] financially or otherwise responsible for the declarant's medical care, or an employee of any such person or institution.

Witness: X_____ Address _____
Witness: X_____ Address _____

Massachusetts: Recommended sample Living Will form is on pp. 51-3.

Michigan: Recommended sample Living Will form is on pp. 51-3.

Minnesota
Health Care Declaration

NOTICE:

This is an important legal document. Before signing this document, you should know these important facts:

(a) This document gives your health care provider or your designated proxy the power and guidance to make health care decisions according to your wishes when you are in a terminal condition and cannot do so. This document may include what kind of treatment you want or do not want and under what circumstances you want these decisions to be made. You may state where you want or do not want to receive any treatment.

(b) If you name a proxy in this document and that person agrees to serve as your proxy, that person has a duty to act consistently with your wishes. If the proxy does not know your wishes, the proxy has the duty to act in your best interests. If you do not name a proxy, your health care providers have a duty to act consistently with your instructions and/or tell you that they are unwilling to do so.

(c) This document will remain valid and in effect until and unless you amend or revoke it. Review this document periodically to make sure it continues to reflect your preferences. You may amend or revoke the declaration at any time by notifying your health care providers.

(d) Your named proxy has the same right as you have to examine your medical records and to consent to their disclosure for purposes relating to your health care or insurance unless you limit this right in this document.

(e) If there is anything in this document that you do not understand, you should ask for professional help to have it explained to you.

To My family, Doctors and All Those
Concerned with My Care

I, _____, being an adult of sound mind, willfully and voluntarily make this statement as a directive to be followed if I am in a terminal condition and become unable to participate in decisions regarding my health care. I understand that my health care providers are legally bound to act consistently with my wishes, within the limits of reasonable medical practice and other applicable law. I also understand that I have the right to make medical and health care decisions for myself as long as I am able to do so and to revoke this declaration at any time.

(1) The following are my feelings and wishes regarding my health care *(you may state the circumstances under which this declaration applies)*:

_____

_____

(2) I particularly want to have all appropriate health care that will help in the following ways *(you may give instructions for care you do want)*:

_____
_____
_____

(3) I particularly do not want the following *(you may list specific treatment you do not want in certain circumstances)*:

_____
_____
_____

(4) I particularly want to have the following kinds of life-sustaining treatment if I am diagnosed to have a terminal condition *(you may list the specific types of life-sustaining treatment you do want if you have a terminal condition)*:

_____
_____
_____

(5) I particularly do not want the following kinds of life-sustaining treatment if I am diagnosed to have a terminal condition *(you may list the specific types of life-sustaining treatment that you do not want if you have a terminal condition)*:

_____
_____
_____

(6) I recognize that if I reject artificially administered sustenance, then I may die of dehydration or malnutrition rather than from my illness or injury. The following are my feelings and wishes regarding artificially administered sustenance should I have a terminal condition *(you may indicate whether you wish to receive food and fluids given to you in some other way than by mouth if you have a terminal condition)*:

_____
_____
_____

(7) Thoughts I feel are relevant to my instructions. *(You may, but need not, give your religious beliefs, philosophy, or other personal values you feel are important. You may also state preferences concerning the location of your care)*:

_____
_____

(8) PROXY DESIGNATION. *(If you wish, you may name someone to see that your wishes are carried out, but you do not have to do this. You may also wish to name a proxy without including specific instructions regarding your care. If you name a proxy you should discuss your wishes with that person)*:

If I become unable to communicate my instructions, I designate the following person(s) [named below] to act on my behalf [as proxy] consistently with my instructions, if any, as stated in this document. Unless I write instructions that limit my proxy's authority, my proxy has full power and authority to make health care decisions for me. If a guardian or conservator of the person is to be appointed for me, I nominate my proxy named in this document to act as guardian or conservator of my person.

Name (of the designated proxy): _____

Address: _____

Phone Number: _____

Relationship: (If any) _____

    If the person I have named above refuses or is unable to act on my behalf, or if I revoke that person's authority to act as my proxy, I authorize the following person to do so:

Name: _____

Address: _____

Phone Number: _____

Relationship: (If any) _____

    I understand that I have the right to revoke the appointment of the person named above to act on my behalf at any time by communicating that decision to the proxy or to my health care provider.

SIGNED: ✗_____ Date:_____

STATE OF_____

COUNTY OF_____

Subscribed, sworn to, and acknowledged before me, by _____,
on this _____day of _____, 19 ___.

_____
(NOTARY PUBLIC)

OR:

(Sign and date here in the presence of two adult witnesses, neither of whom is entitled to any part of your estate under a will or by operation of law, and neither of whom is your proxy.)

    I certify that the declarant voluntarily signed this declaration in my presence and that the declarant is personally known to me. I am not named as a proxy by this declaration, and to the best of my knowledge, I am not entitled to any part of the estate of the declarant under a will or by operation of law.

Witness ✗_____

Address _____

Witness ✗_____

Address _____

**Reminder: Keep the signed original with your personal papers.
Give signed copies to your doctors, family, and proxy.**

Mississippi
Declaration

Declaration made on _____ *(date)*
by _____ *(name)*
of _____ *(address)*
_____ *(Social Security No.)*

I, _____, being of sound mind, declare that if [at] any time I should suffer a terminal physical condition which causes me severe distress or unconsciousness, and my physician, with the concurrence of two (2) other physicians, believes that there is no expectation of my regaining consciousness or a state of health that is meaningful to me and but for the use of life-sustaining mechanisms my death would be imminent, I desire that the mechanisms be withdrawn so that I may die naturally. However, if I have been diagnosed as pregnant and that diagnosis is known to my physician, this declaration shall have no force or effect during the course of my pregnancy. I further declare that this declaration shall be honored by my family and my physician as the final expression of my desires concerning the manner in which I die.

Signed ✗ _____
(Declarant)

I hereby witness this declaration and attest that:
   (1) I personally know the Declarant and believe the Declarant to be of sound mind.
   (2) To the best of my knowledge, at the time of the execution of the declaration, I:
      (a) Am not related to the Declarant by blood or marriage.
      (b) Do not have any claim on the estate of the Declarant.
      (c) Am not entitled to any portion of the Declarant's estate by any will or by operation of law.
      (d) Am not a physician attending the Declarant or a person employed by a physician attending the Declarant.

Witness ✗_____
Address _____
_____ Soc. Sec. No._____

Witness ✗_____
Address _____
_____ Soc. Sec. No._____

[Mississippi law requires that, in order for this Living Will to be considered valid, a copy of it be mailed, along with a $10 filing fee, to the State Division of Public Health Statistics, because under the Mississippi procedure it is required that in order to act on your Declaration, your physician must receive a certified copy of it from the state Division of Public Health Statistics, along with a statement certifying that you have not filed a revocation with the department. So, here's where to send a copy to, along with the $10 filing fee:
      Division of Public Health Statistics
      P. O. Box 1700
      Jackson, MS 39215-1700]

Missouri: Recommended sample Living Will form is on pp. 51-3.

Montana: Recommended sample Living Will form is on pp. 51-3.

Nebraska: Recommended sample Living Will form is on pp. 51-3.

Nevada: Recommended sample Living Will form is on pp. 51-3.

New Hampshire: Recommended sample Living Will form is on pp. 51-3.

New Jersey: Recommended sample Living Will form is on pp. 51-3.

New Mexico: Recommended sample Living Will form is on pp. 51-3.

New York: Recommended sample Living Will form is on pp. 51-3.

North Carolina
Declaration of a Desire for a Natural Death

I, _____, being of sound mind, desire that my life not be prolonged by extraordinary means if my condition is determined to be terminal and incurable. I am aware and understand that this writing authorizes a physician to withhold or discontinue extraordinary means.

Other directions:_____

_____

_____

_____

This the _____ day of _____19____.

Signature X _____
(Declarant)

I hereby state that the declarant, _____, being of sound mind signed the above declaration in my presence and that I am not related to the declarant by blood or marriage and that I do not know or have a reasonable expectation that I would be entitled to any portion of the estate of the declarant under any existing will or codicil of the declarant or as an heir under the intestate Succession Act if the declarant died on this date without a will. I also state that I am not the declarant's attending physician or an employee of the declarant's attending physician, or an employee of a health facility in which the declarant is a patient or an employee of a nursing home or any group-care home where the declarant resides. I further state that I do not now have any claim against the declarant.

Witness X_____
Witness X_____

[In order for this document to be legally valid in the state of North Carolina it must be sworn to before a state Superior Court clerk or a North Carolina notary public.]

Certificate
I, _____, Clerk (assistant Clerk) of Superior Court or Notary Public *(circle one as appropriate)* for _____, County hereby certify that _____, the declarant, appeared before me and swore to me and to the witnesses in my presence that this instrument is his Declaration of a Desire for a Natural Death, and that he had willingly and voluntarily made and executed it as

his free act and deed for the purpose expressed in it.

I further certify that _____ and _____,

witnesses, appeared before me and swore that they witnessed_____,

the declarant, sign the attached declaration, believing him to be of sound mind; and also swore that at the time they witnessed the declaration (i) they were not related within the third degree to the declarant or to the declarant's spouse, and (ii) they did not know or have a reasonable expectation that they would be entitled to any portion of the estate of the declarant upon the declarant's death under any will of the declarant or codicil thereto then existing or under the Intestate Succession Act as it provides at that time, and (iii) they were not a physician attending the declarant or an employee of an attending physician or an employee of a health care facility in which the declarant was a patient or an employee of a nursing home or any group-care home in which the declarant is a resident, and (iv) they did not have a claim against the declarant. I further certify that I am satisfied as to the genuineness and due execution of the declaration.

This _____ day _____19_____.

Clerk (Assistant Clerk) or Superior Court of Notary Public *(circle one as appropriate)* for the County of _____.

North Dakota
Declaration

Declaration made this _____day of _____ *(month, year).*

I, _____, being at least eighteen years of age and of sound mind, willfully and voluntarily make known my desire that my life must not be artificially prolonged under the circumstances set forth below, and do hereby declare:

1. If at any time I should have an incurable condition caused by injury, disease or illness certified to be a terminal condition by two physicians, and where the application of life prolonging treatment would serve only to artificially prolong the process of my dying and my attending physician determines that my death is imminent whether or not life prolonging treatment is utilized, I direct that such treatment be withheld or withdrawn, and that I be permitted to die naturally.

2. In the absence of my ability to give directions regarding the use of such life-prolonging treatment, it is my intention that this declaration be honored by my family and physicians as the final expression of my legal right to refuse medical or surgical treatment and accept the consequences of that refusal, which is death.

3. If I have been diagnosed as pregnant and that diagnosis is known to my physician, this declaration is not effective during the course of my pregnancy.

4. 1 understand the full import of this declaration and I am emotionally and mentally competent to make this declaration.

5. 1 understand that I may revoke this declaration at any time.

Signed ✗ _____
                          (Declarant)

City, County, and State of Residence _____

The declarant has been personally known to me and I believe the declarant to be of sound mind. I am not related to the declarant by blood or marriage, nor would I be entitled to any portion of the declarant's estate upon the declarant's death. I am not the declarant's attending physician, [or] a person who has a claim against any portion of the state upon the declarant's death, or a person financially responsible for the declarant's medical care.

Witness ✗_____

Witness ✗_____

Ohio: Recommended sample Living Will form is on pp. 51-3.

Oklahoma
Directive to Physicians

Directive made this _____ day of _____ *(month, year)*.

I, _____, being of sound mind and twenty-one (21) years of age or older, willfully and voluntarily make known my desire that my life shall not be artificially prolonged under the circumstances set forth below, and do hereby declare:

(1) If at any time I should have an incurable irreversible condition caused by injury, disease, or illness certified to be a terminal condition by two physicians, I direct that procedures be withheld or withdrawn and that I be permitted to die naturally, if the application of life-sustaining procedures would serve only to artificially prolong the moment of my death and my attending physician determines my death is imminent whether or not life-sustaining procedures are utilized;

Other directions:_____

_____

_____

_____

(2) In the absence of my ability to give directions regarding the use of such life-sustaining procedures, it is my intention that this directive shall be honored by my family and physicians as the final expression of my legal right to refuse medical or surgical treatment and accept the consequences of such refusal;

(3) If I have been diagnosed as pregnant and that diagnosis is known to my physician, this directive shall have no force or effect during the course of my pregnancy;

(4) I have been diagnosed and notified as having a terminal condition by_____,
M.D. or D.O., whose address is _____ and whose telephone number is _____.

I understand that if I have not filled in the name and address of the physician, it shall be presumed that I did not have a terminal condition when I made out this directive;

(5) This directive shall be in effect until it is revoked;

(6) I understand the full import of this directive and am emotionally and mentally competent to make this directive; and

(7) I understand that I may revoke this directive at any time.

Signed ✗ _____
(Declarant)

City, County and State of Residence _____

The declarant has been personally known to me and I believe [the] said declarant to be of sound mind. I am twentyone (21) years of age or older, I am not related to the declarant by blood or marriage, nor would I be entitled to any portion of the estate of the declarant upon the death of said declarant, nor am I the attending physician of the declarant or any employee of the attending physician or a health care facility in which the declarant is a patient, or a patient in the health care facility in which the declarant is a patient, nor am I financially responsible for the medical care of the declarant, or any person who has a claim against any portion of the estate of the declarant upon the death of the declarant.

Witness ✗_____

Witness ✗_____

STATE OF OKLAHOMA _____)

) SS.:

COUNTY OF _____)

Before me, the undersigned authority, on this day personally appeared
_____ (declarant)
_____ (witness)

whose names are subscribed to the foregoing instrument in their respective capacities, and, all of [the] said persons being by me duly sworn, the declarant declared to me and to the said witnesses in my presence that the said instrument is his or her "Directive to Physicians," and that the declarant had willingly and voluntarily made and executed it as the free act and deed of the declarant for the purposes therein expressed.

The foregoing instrument was acknowledged before me this _____ day of _____, 19 _____ .

Signed 𝘟_____

Notary Public in and for _____ County, Oklahoma
My Commission Expires _____ day of _____, 19 _____ .

Oregon
Directive to Physician

Directive made this _____ day _____ (month, year).

I , _____ , being of sound mind, willfully and voluntarily make known my desire that my life shall not be artificially prolonged under the circumstances set forth below and do hereby declare:

1. If at any time I should have an incurable injury, disease or illness certified to be a terminal condition by two physicians, one of whom is the attending physician, and where the application of life-sustaining procedures would serve only to artificially prolong the moment of my death and where my physician determines that my death is imminent whether or not life-sustaining procedures are utilized, I direct that such procedures be withheld or withdrawn, and that I be permitted to die naturally.

2. In the absence of my ability to give directions regarding the use of such life-sustaining procedures, it is my intention that this directive shall be honored by my family and physician(s) as the final expression of my legal right to refuse medical or surgical treatment and accept the consequences from such refusal.

3. I understand the full import of this directive and I am emotionally and mentally competent to make this directive.

Signed 𝘟_____
                                    (declarant)

City, County and State of Residence _____

I hereby witness this directive and attest that
(1) I personally know the Declarant and believe the Declarant to be of sound mind.
(2) To the best of my knowledge, at the time of the execution of this directive, I:

(a) Am not related to the Declarant by blood or marriage,

(b) Do not have any claim on the estate of the Declarant,

(c) Am not entitled to any portion of the Declarant's estate by any will or by operation of law, and

(d) Am not the physician attending the Declarant or a person employed by a physician attending the Declarant or a person employed by a health facility in which the Declarant is a patient.

(3) 1 understand that if I have not witnessed this directive in good faith I may be responsible for any damages that arise out of giving this directive its intended effect.

Witness ✗_____

Witness ✗_____

Pennsylvania: Recommended sample Living Will form is on pp. 51-3.

South Carolina
Declaration of a Desire for a Natural Death

State of South Carolina,

County of _____) ss.:

I,_____,a resident of and domiciled in the City of
_____ , County of _____ , State of South Carolina, make this
Declaration this _____ day of _____, 19 _____ .

I willfully and voluntarily make known my desire that no life-sustaining procedures be used to prolong my dying if my condition is terminal, and I hereby do declare:

If at any time I have an incurable injury, disease or illness certified to be a terminal condition by two physicians who have personally examined me, one of whom is my attending physician, and the physicians have determined that my death will occur without the use of life-sustaining procedures and where the application of life-sustaining procedures would serve only to prolong the dying process, I direct that such procedures be withheld or withdrawn, and that I be permitted to die naturally with only the administration of medication or the performance of any medical procedure necessary to provide me with comfort care.

Other directions: _____

_____

_____

_____

In the absence of my ability to give directions regarding the use of such life-sustaining procedures, it is my intention that this Declaration be honored by my family and physicians as the final expression of my legal right to refuse medical or surgical treatment and I accept the consequences from such refusal.

I am aware that this Declaration authorizes a physician to withhold or withdraw life-sustaining procedures. I am emotionally and mentally competent to make this Declaration.

This Declaration may be revoked by the declarant, without regard to his physical or mental condition.

(1) By being defaced, torn, obliterated, or otherwise destroyed by the declarant or by some person in the presence of and by the direction of the declarant.

(2) By a written revocation signed and dated by the declarant expressing his or her intent to revoke. The revocation shall become effective only upon communication to the attending physician by the declarant or by a person acting on behalf of the declarant. The attending physician shall record in the patient's medical record the time and date when he received notification of the written revocation.

(3) By a verbal expression by the declarant of his intent to revoke the declaration. The revocation shall become effective only upon communication to the attending physician by the declarant. The attending physician shall record in the patient's medical record the time, date and place of the revocation and the time, date, and place, if different, of when he received notification of the revocation.

Signed ✗ _____
(declarant)

Affidavit

State of_____)
) ss.:
County of _____)

We, _____,
_____and_____,
the witnesses whose names are signed to the foregoing Declaration, dated the _____ day of _____, 19 _____ , being first duly sworn, do hereby declare to the undersigned authority that the declaration was on that date signed by the said declarant as and for his *Declaration of a Desire for a Natural Death* in our presence and we, at his request and in his presence, and in the presence of each other, did thereunto subscribe our names as witnesses on that date. The declarant is personally known to us and we believe him to be of sound mind. None of us is disqualified as a witness to this Declaration by any provision of the South Carolina Death With Dignity Act. None of us is related to the declarant by blood or marriage; nor directly financially responsible for the declarant's medical care; nor entitled to any portion of the declarant's estate upon his decease, whether under any will or as an heir by intestate succession; nor the beneficiary of a life insurance policy of the declarant; nor the declarant's attending physician; nor an employee of such attending physician; nor a person who has claim against the declarant's decedent's estate as of this time. No more than one of us is an employee of a health facility in which the declarant is a patient. If the declarant is a patient in a hospital or skilled or intermediate care nursing facility at the date of execution of this declaration at least one of us is an ombudsman designated by the State Ombudsman, Office of the Governor.

Witness ✗_____
Witness ✗_____
Witness ✗_____

SUBSCRIBED, SWORN TO, AND ACKNOWLEDGED BEFORE ME by _____, the declarant, and subscribed and sworn to before me by _____
and _____ the witnesses, this _____day of _____, 19 ____ .

_____
(Notary Public for)
   My commission expires: _____
      [SEAL]

Tennessee: Recommended sample Living Will form is on pp. 51-3.
Texas: Recommended sample Living Will form is on pp. 51-3.

Utah
Directive to Physicians and Providers of Medical Services
(Pursuant to Section 75-2-1104, UCA)

This directive is made this _____ day of _____ 19 _____ .

1. I, _____, being of sound mind, willfully and voluntarily make known my desire that my life not be artifically prolonged by life-sustaining procedures except as I may otherwise provide in this directive.

2. I declare that if at any time I should have an injury, disease, or illness, which is certified in writing to be terminal condition by two physicians who have personally examined me, and in the opinion of those physicians the application of life-sustaining procedures would serve only to unnaturally prolong the moment of my death and to unnaturally postpone or prolong the dying process, I direct that these procedures be withheld or withdrawn and my death be permitted to occur naturally.

3. I expressly intend this directive to be a final expression of my legal right to refuse medical or surgical treatment and to accept the consequences from this refusal which shall remain in effect notwithstanding my future inability to give current medical directions to treating physicians and other providers of medical services.

4. I understand that the term "life-sustaining procedures" does not include the administration of medication or sustenance, or the performance of any medical procedure deemed necessary to provide comfort care, or to alleviate pain, except to the extent I specify below that any of these procedures be considered life-sustaining:

[Author's note: At this point in the Utah Living Will you may insert any specific directions you have regarding particular types of care or treatment you might not want under certain circumstances. For instance, you might say that you would not, in accordance with the principles of the American Medical Association, want to be tube fed if you were diagnosed as being in a persistent vegetative state.]

5. I reserve the right to give current medical directions to physicians and other providers of medical services so long as I am able, even though these directions may conflict with the above written directive that life-sustaining procedures be withheld or withdrawn.

6. I understand the full import of this directive and declare that I am emotionally and mentally competent to make this directive.

Signed ✗ _____
                     (declarant's signature)

City, county and state of residence_____

We, [the] witnesses, certify that each of us is 18 years of age or older and each personally witnessed the declarant sign or direct the signing of this directive; that we are acquainted with declarant and believe him to be of sound mind; that the declarant's desires are as expressed above; that neither of us is a person who signed the above directive on behalf of the declarant; that we are not related to the declarant by blood or marriage nor are we entitled to any portion of declarant's estate according to the laws of intestate succession of this state or under any will or codicil of declarant; that we are not directly financially responsible for declarant's medical care; and that we are not agents of any health care facility in which declarant may be a patient at the time of signing this directive.

✗_____   ✗_____
     (signature of witness)   (signature of witness)

_____   _____
     (address of witness)   (address of witness)

Vermont: Recommended sample Living Will form is on pp. 51-3.

Virginia: Recommended sample Living Will form is on pp. 51-3.

Washington
Directive to Physician

Directive made this _____ day _____ *(month, year)*.

I, _____ , being of sound mind, willfully and voluntarily make known my desire that my life shall not be artificially prolonged under the circumstances set forth below, and do hereby declare that:

(a) If at any time I should have an incurable injury, disease, or illness certified to be a terminal condition by two physicians, and where the application of life-sustaining procedures would serve only to artificially prolong the moment of my death and where my physician determines that my death is imminent whether or not life-sustaining procedures are utilized, I direct that such procedures be withheld or withdrawn, and that I be permitted to die naturally.

(b) In the absence of my ability to give directions regarding the use of such life-sustaining procedures, it is my intention that this directive shall be honored by my family and physician(s) as the final expression of my legal right to refuse medical or surgical treatment and I accept the consequences from such refusal.

(c) If I have been diagnosed as pregnant and that diagnosis is known to my physician, this directive shall have no force or effect during the course of my pregnancy.

(d) I understand the full import of this directive and I am emotionally and mentally competent to make this directive.

Other directions: _____
_____
_____
_____

Signed ✗ _____
(declarant)

City, county and State of Residence _____

The declarer has been personally known to me and I believe him/her to be of sound mind.

Witness ✗_____
(print & sign name)

Witness ✗_____
(print & sign name)

West Virginia: Recommended sample Living Will form is on pp. 51-3.

Wisconsin
Declaration to Physicians

Declaration made this _____ day of _____ *(month, year)*.

1. I , _____ , being of sound mind, willfully and voluntarily state my desire that my dying may not be artificially prolonged if I have an incurable injury or illness certified to be a terminal condition by 2 (two) physicians who have personally examined me, one of whom is my attending physician, and if the physicians have determined that my death is imminent, so that the application of life-sustaining procedures would serve only to prolong artificially the dying process. Under these circumstances, I direct that life-sustaining procedures be withheld or withdrawn and that I be permitted to die naturally, with only:

    a. The continuation of nutritional support and fluid maintenance; and

    b. The alleviation of pain by administering medication or other medical procedure.

Other instructions: _____
_____
_____
_____

2. If I am unable to give directions regarding the use of life-sustaining procedures, I intend that my family and physician honor this declaration as the final expression of my legal right to refuse medical or surgical treatment and to accept the consequences from this refusal.

3. If I have been diagnosed as pregnant and the physician knows of this diagnosis, this declaration has no effect during the course of my pregnancy.

4. This declaration takes effect immediately.

I understand this declaration and I am emotionally and mentally competent to make this declaration.

Signed ✗ _____
                                         (declarant)

Address _____

I know the declarant personally and I believe him or her to be of sound mind. I am not related to the declarant by blood or marriage, and am not entitled to the declarant's estate under any will of declarant. I am neither the declarant's attending physician, the attending nurse, the attending medical staff, nor an employee of the attending physician or of the inpatient health care facility in which the declarant may be a patient and I have no claim against the declarant's estate at this time, except that I am not a health care provider who is involved in the medical care of the declarant, I may be an employee of the inpatient health care facility regardless of whether or not the facility may have a claim against the estate of the declarant.

Witness ✗_____
Witness ✗_____

Wyoming: Recommended sample Living Will form is on pp. 51-3.

Appendix D

WILL SUBSTITUTES: CERTAIN OTHER ESTATE PLANNING METHODS OF PASSING ON PROPERTY

A. What is a Will Substitute?

One question that often arises in the general subject of estate planning (of which Will-making is, of course, just one important part), is whether the Will is the only legal method by which one's property and affairs could be disposed of after death.

Is it? Of course not. There are many other methods available, each with varying advantages and disadvantages, and some more suited to particular needs, objectives, and individuals than others. Collectively, such methods are often referred to as "Will substitutes" mainly because the same provisions can be incorporated in many of them as can be put in a Will. And, often, much like the Will, these substitutes have the effect of enabling an estate to avoid or reduce the probate process and the associated costs and expenses or taxes.

Will substitutes include the following instruments: revocable trusts, jointly held property, United States Savings bonds, life insurance, employment benefits, and others.

B. Some Principal Categories of Will Substitutes

The following are among the major Will substitutes:

1. The Revocable Trust

Briefly, a trust is a written agreement which has the legal effect of separating the ownership of the trust maker's property into two parts—one part gives the legal title (or management) of the trust property to one person or institution, and the other part gives the beneficial ownership of the property to another. Broadly speaking, trusts are classified into two main categories: *i) the Living Trust,* which is one that is created during the lifetime of the trust maker; and *ii) the Testamentary Trust,* which is one created by Will and takes effect only after the death of the maker.

Now, within the living trusts category, there are again two basic types — the *irrevocable* trust (a living trust which cannot be changed or cancelled by the maker), and the *revocable* trust, which is a living trust that can be changed or cancelled by the maker during his lifetime.

In a revocable trust case, withdrawal of any trust assets from the trust, or the complete cancellation of the trust, can be made at any time at the request of the maker, except in certain special cases—e.g., where the trust maker has surrendered the power of revocation to another person. In the typical revocable living trust, the trust maker (he's also known as the trust "creator" or "settlor" or "grantor") draws up the trust agreement transferring property to a named trustee. The person or bank named to act as the trustee, is given the legal title, possession and management of the trust assets. The trust agreement usually provides for the trustee to pay the maker the income from the trust during his (the maker's) lifetime, and perhaps a part of the principal of the trust. The agreement would also give the maker the sole power to amend or revoke the trust or change the trustee at any time.

Under trust laws, once the maker of a trust dies, the trust becomes irrevocable: the terms of the trust at the time cannot be changed thereafter. Those terms would continue to operate for the benefit of the beneficiaries or other persons named in the trust. Hence, the effect becomes at that point, very much the same as though the property were being distributed under a Will. The trustee would, however, continue to retain control and management of the trust assets. And therefore, the trust assets do not have to pass through any estate administration process with the usual probate expenses and delays involved.[1]

---

[1]It should be noted, however, that trust creations do not necessarily come cost-free; there are costs associated with the actual creation and then the administration of trusts, principally the trustee's fees and charges for managing the trust assets during and after the maker's lifetime. For all about an alternative low-cost or cost-free way of creating and managing a revocable living trust, see *How To Properly Plan Your 'Total' Estate With A Living Trust Without The Lawyers' Fees,* by Benji Anosike (Do-It-Yourself Legal Publishers).

2. Jointly Held Property

This is one of the more common kinds of "Will Substitute." Where any property or assets (e.g. savings accounts, securities, real estate) are owned by two persons as joint tenants with "the right of survivorship" provisions, that property or asset will generally pass directly to the surviving partner by the operation of law. One distinct advantage of having property in joint names is that it provides an immediate, automatic transfer of title to the survivor. However, there are some important disadvantages to joint ownership arrangements. For example, both partners may die in a common accident thereby throwing the property up for grabs — unless, of course, there's a good Will available which makes provisions for alternative disposition of the estate in the event of such a contingency. Secondly, joint ownership arrangements may be a problem where the family relationship ceases to be harmonious, e.g., in a divorce situation.[2]

3. United States Bonds

When U.S. savings bonds are held in the names of two persons as co-owners, the surviving co-owner becomes the sole owner of the bonds on the death of the other. And when the bond is held in the name of one person and payable on death to another person, the person named as beneficiary becomes the sole owner upon the death of the person in whose name it's held. In each instance, the bond will pass **directly** to the parties, and no Will (or any other instrument) is required in order to direct its distribution.

4. Life Insurance

Life Insurance proceeds are always paid directly to the beneficiary named in the policy. However, when the proceeds are payable to the insured himself, or to his "estate" or "personal representative"—a provision almost universally considered among estate planning experts to be an ill-advised and major mistake to make—then the proceeds will be treated as part of the decedent's estate and be subject to distribution as such.

> NOTE: One unusual virtue of insurance, is that even when the proceeds are payable to the estate of the insured, they are exempt from the claims of his creditors; and when the proceeds are payable to the spouse of the insured, they are exempt from the claims of the spouse's creditors.[3]

5. Employment Benefits

Various types of employment-related benefits are almost always paid directly to the person designated as the beneficiary in the employment contract, except in instances where the benefits are to be paid to the employee's estate—i.e., where a person (an employee) has for some reason designated his "estate" as the beneficiary. Examples of employment-related benefits would include the following: any wages, vacation pay or fringe benefits to which the decedent is entitled; life, health or accident insurance plans; retirement, pension or profit-sharing plans; stock option plans; deferred compensation or union benefits, and the like.

C. Should You Do Without a Will if You Have a Will Substitute?

The answer is NEVER! Sure, various Will substitutes have many virtues and advantages of sorts. But there should be no misunderstanding whatsoever about-one basic fact: *no Will substitute could adequately substitute for or take the place of a good, properly drawn-up, up-to-date Will.* One reason this is so is that Will substitutes do not always suit the needs and circumstances of everyone. Their suitability would often depend on a person's particular circumstances — the amount and nature of his assets and liabilities, the status of his family, and what exactly he needs or prefers. In all you do, the central point to remember is that *Will substitutes should always be used to supplement and coordinate the provisions of a Will — not as a total substitute for it.*

Will substitutes usually do not always work out in doing what they are intended for. Hence they often invite unnecessary lawsuits. Take, for example, the jointly held property. Suppose a man dies, leaving a savings account that is held jointly in his name and his brother's name. Now, suppose the decedent's brother

---

[2]For more elaborate discussions of the pros and cons of the use of these and other devices as probate avoidance and estate planning devices, see *How To Properly Plan Your 'Total' Estate With A Living Trust, Without The Lawyers' Fees,* by Benji Anosike (Do-It-Yourself Legal Publishers).

[3]Ibid.

claims the savings account as his own property being that he's the surviving joint owner. In such a situation, it's not unusual to find that he will find himself challenged by other relatives. The other relatives may argue, for example, that the decedent had not really intended to give the brother the decedent's own right of a joint owner, but had added his name to the decedent's account solely for convenience — in order, merely, to allow the brother to obtain funds for the decedent's use during his life. Who gains then? No one! The matter will be thrown into court and may drag on and on forever at great expense. That's just one illustration of why the so-called "Will substitutes" may not be taken literally mean that it could take the place of a good, well-drafted Will (or, for that matter, of other estate planning devices)!!

> **NOTE:** For more on this issue, see Section E of Chapter 2, "Suppose You Have All Your Property In Joint Names & Trusts, Is A Will Still Necessary?" (p. 8)

D. A Word of Caution on Using Will Substitutes

When Will substitutes are used with a Will, it is absolutely essential that their relationship with one another, and with the Will itself, be carefully worked out and COORDINATED. For instance, unless a father's Will provides that death taxes be paid from his probate property, a home that a father and son own together in joint names would be required to bear a share of the estate and inheritance taxes upon the father's death. Similarly, a decedent may have specifically taken out a life insurance for the purpose of employing the proceeds to pay off estate taxes, debts and funeral expenses at his death. However, what if (as it usually happens) the insurance is made payable to a beneficiary other than the estate of the decedent? The executor may not then be entitled to get the insurance proceeds and would have to find funds from other sources to meet such obligations.

There is one famous story that illustrates the great importance of carefully coordinating the relationship of these documents. A man with an independently wealthy wife had drawn up a Will with his wife's consent leaving "my entire estate to my son, Sam." However, at the man's death, all his son was legally able to receive was the decedent's golf clubs and a watch! Why? Because it turned out that the man's "entire estate" consisted of assets which were already assigned or held in joint names with other parties: his home, held in joint names with his wife; two bank accounts, one held jointly with his wife, and the other in trust for his mother; life insurance payable to his wife; and a death benefit from his employer for which he had named his wife as beneficiary. *The deceased father did not, in short, realize that the "entire estate" clause he had entered in his Will was not COORDINATED and made compatible with the terms of his Will substitutes so as to avoid such a ludicrous overlap!*

Appendix E
PROBATE PROCEDURES: CARRYING OUT THE PROVISIONS OF THE WILL WHEN A TESTATOR DIES*

What happens when a person who made a Will dies? Who sees to it that what the testator provided for in the Will are carried out and how?

Issues of this sort — called "probate procedures" in legal jargon — are of course a separate matter, one step removed from the primary subject matter of this manual. Probate matters do not arise until the testator is dead and gone. Probate and estate procedures proper, are clearly beyond the scope of the present manual, and those who wish to learn the details of such procedures are strongly advised to consult the sister volume to this manual also published by the same publisher as this volume and entitled, *"HOW TO PROBATE, ADMINISTER AND SETTLE AN ESTATE YOURSELF WITHOUT A LAWYER"* authored by Benji O. Anosike. However, because of the clear relatedness of probate to the whole issue of Will-making, this Appendix will be devoted to some basic pointers on the general principles of probate.

A. What is the Probate System?

The probate procedures are, in brief, the whole business of managing ("administering") the property and affairs of a dead person under the supervision of a Probate or Surrogate Court. When a person dies and leaves some property of any kind or size behind, there's always this question: who is lawfully entitled to inherit the decedent's estate? Often, it is not unusual to find a long list of relatives, real or otherwise, coming from near and far to lay claims to a share of the estate. This, say the legal professionals, is the fundamental reason why there must be a probate system — an often costly and lengthy process, particularly when no good Will (or other probate-avoidance tools) exist. In theory, at least, the object of probate is to give the court a temporary supervision of the control and management of the decedent's estate so as to protect it from the possibility of misuse, and to eventually ensure that the decedent's heirs, creditors, and others who are rightfully entitled to the estate would get it.

B. Does the Court Physically Administer
The Decedent's Estate?

No. Strictly speaking, the probate function of the court is generally supervisory — it supervises the work of the Executor (or the Administrator), who is the one who actually does the managing work of the decedent's estate. In other words, when a person dies leaving a Will, the person (or institution) who must assume the direct responsibility of seeing that the provisions of his Will are carried out is the person designated in his Will to act as the executor or executrix. The court would merely watch over what he or she does, to make sure that the responsibilities are properly carried out.

When the decedent leaves a Will, the administration and probate functions of the executor are generally more simplified (and less costly); unlike what happens in no-Will situations, the provisions of the Will are there to guide the executor along. He would know, for example, where and how the decedent wishes to be buried, the nature and locations of his assets or indebtedness, who his beneficiaries are, and the like. Following the instructions of the testator in his Will as closely as possible, therefore, the probate responsibilities of the executor ought to go fast and smoothly.

---

*For detailed treatment of this topic, see *"How To Probate, Administer And Settle An Estate Yourself Without A Lawyer,"* published by the Do-It-Yourself Legal Publishers.

C. The duties of the Executor In Carrying Out The Provisions Of The Will

Figure E-1 (see pp. 113) fairly well illustrates, graphically, the typical estate settlement and probate process. Listed below are the principal duties and responsibilities of the executor following the death of the testator. Basically, he (or she) is required to do the following:

1. Locate the Will. (It may have been placed in the testator's home, his safe deposit box, his attorney's or accountant's office, in the probate court clerk's office, kept with the executor himself, etc.)

2. Carry out any special instructions in the Will concerning funeral and burial arrangements, if any.

3. Probate the Will before the Probate or Surrogate Court — that is, submit it to the court and show proof that what he has submitted is truly the Will of the dead person, actually made and signed by him or her.

4. Be officially confirmed by the court to act as the executor, and obtain his **_"Letters Testamentary"_** (the formal document of authority) authorizing him to act as the executor for the decedent. (See a sample of one variant of the Letters Testamentary used in New York's Kings County at p. 114)

5. Open the decedent's safe deposit box, if any, and make a record of its contents.

6. Ascertain all the personal or real property of the decedent and assemble them so that none would be lost, misused or overlooked; prepare an inventory of such property and have them properly appraised for their proper value.

7. Collect the proceeds of assets like life insurance, pension, dividends, interests, rents, veteran and social security benefits, rent or utility deposits, and the like, as applicable.

8. Ascertain all debts owed to the decedent, if any, and collect them.

9. Arrange (if applicable) to have the decedent's business or investments continued, liquidated, or sold — depending on the decedent's instructions in his Will.

10. Set aside any property that is exempt from administration for the benefit of the family or surviving spouse, or maintenance funds for the family (the "widow's allowance"), and provide it to the family to prevent undue financial hardship to the family during the estate administration period.

11. Publish or otherwise give proper notice to decedent's creditors for submission of their claims against the estate, if any.

12. Pay off the decedent's funeral expenses, the lawful debts, taxes or claims against his estate, and the expenses incurred in administering his estate. (In insufficient asset estates, he may have to sell certain estate assets to meet the estate obligations.)

13. Defend the estate in court, if anyone should contest the Will or sue the decedent's estate for whatever reason.

14. Assemble the beneficiaries of the estate and distribute the balance of the estate (what is left after paying off the estate debts and administration expenses, etc.) to them in accordance with the provisions of the Will.

15. Submit a final accounting of his services — detailed statements of receipts and disbursements for the estate — to the court and obtain a formal discharge as executor.

D. How Long Does Probate and Estate Administration Take?

As a rule, lawyers who make a living out of probate work have long been reputed to have a habit of unnecessarily prolonging the probate procedures way beyond what it should legitimately take. (They get paid, of course, according to the amount of time they could claim they spent on the "probate work"!!)

Edward E. Colby, a concerned California attorney who wrote _Everything You've Always Wanted to Know About the Law But Couldn't Afford to Ask,_ makes this complaint of the probate court redtape: "The time factor is shocking and no one can explain any valid reason for (the) long delays."

Another of the many critics, Harper Hamilton of Boulder, Colorado, who is also an attorney and author, speaks harshly of the "probate rip off" involved in the typical probate process. Hamilton sums it up this way:

> "Typically, if any member of a family wanted to transfer property to other members — during lifetime — it can be done with the ease of signing a piece of paper…simple, easy, a few minutes of your time. No big deal…
>
> But, hold it! Suppose he dies and the SAME property is to be transferred through the 'probate process.'? It will take the typical 'probate' matter one, two, three, five years to complete. You must bear unnecessary probate 'costs,' 'expenses,' delays, court proceedings, and on and on. Why is that?"

The point is that if you go by the "typical" lawyer-managed case, the probate process could take anywhere from as little as a few weeks or months in small-to-medium size estates, to several years. In the larger-than-average estates (those with a gross estate value of over $600,000), the time frame is generally measured in years. But, we'd argue, though, as a practical matter, a period of one year[1]—if properly made use of—should generally be more than enough to complete the normal, average estate administration. This should especially be so where the relatives or beneficiaries readily cooperate with the executor and no unusual number of claims, litigations or contests arise.

E. If my Will is Contested During Probate, Under What Conditions Could the Terms Be Set Aside?

It should first be stated that, in most instances, the terms of the Will would be acceptable to the court as final. Nor are most Wills often contested. However, there are some few instances when the terms of the Will may be contested or, for certain reasons, be set aside or disregarded in assigning distribution rights.

1. One instance would be where a Will fails to provide absolutely anything for the surviving spouse, or for the minor children of the decedent. The inheritance laws of most states provide for the spouse (the same for children in a few states) to receive a certain share of the estate, even if a Will provides otherwise. Such rights are known as the rights of *"election,"* and of *"dower and curtesy."*

2. Another instance would be where a Will proves (or is proved by contesting parties) to be invalid for any number of reasons: undue influence, fraud or duress on the testator; serious mistakes made in the signing of the Will; insanity or lack of mental capacity on the part of the testator <u>at the time</u> of making of the Will, etc. In such instances, the decedent will simply be thought of by the court as one who died without leaving a Will, and his estate will therefore "descend" (be distributed) according to the state's laws of Descent and Distribution.

3. A third instance would be where a decedent dies "partially testate" and "partially intestate" — that is, for example, where some of the testator's property is either not mentioned in the Will or other estate distribution instruments, or is given to a beneficiary who later dies before (or soon after) the testator, and for which no "residuary" provision or alternative beneficiary had been named to inherit the item. When that is the case, that portion of the estate to which the partial intestacy applies will "descend" (be distributed) according to the local law of Descent and Distribution.

4. Finally, those kinds of property which are said to "pass by operation of law" (Appendix D of the manual), are usually governed by the provisions of the "substitute Wills" — the life insurance policy, revocable trust agreement, joint tenancy terms, pension contracts, and the like.

THIS MUCH CAN BE SAID ON THIS QUESTION, HOWEVER, WITH CERTAINTY: *If you diligently follow the prescribed rules and guidelines set forth in this manual (see especially Chapters 4 & 5), in the drafting of your Will, and be sure to avoid the typical "pitfalls" often fallen into even by lawyers and other professionals in the drafting of a Will (see Chapter 7), you can be certain that you shall have drastically reduced the chances of your Will being challenged in the first place—or, at least, being successfully challenged—to almost zero!*

---

[1] The reason it should even be this long is that the probate laws of most states require a "minimum" waiting period of time (usually 6, 9 or 12 months) for completing probate of any kind. Hence, even if every required step is accomplished long before the minimum period, you may still have to wait out a period of time before you may conclude the probate process.

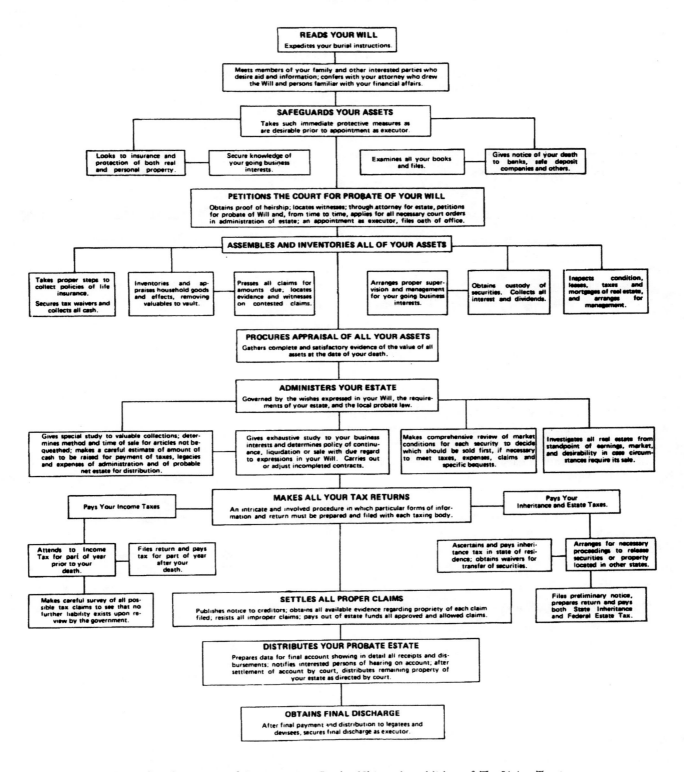

FIGURE E-1
ESTATE EXECUTOR'S DUTIES DURING THE PROBATE PROCESS

Reproduced, courtesy of Contemporary Books (Chicago), publisher of *The Living Trust*,
by Henry W. Abts III, to whom the present author and publisher are deeply indebted.

At Chambers of the Surrogate's
Court of the County of Kings,
State of New York, at the Court house in
said county, on the_____day of
_____, in the year 19_____

PRESENT:

_____ **HONORABLE**
(Name of Presiding Judge)
Surrogate.

PROBATE PROCEEDING, Will
of

_____
John Doe
Deceased

}

**Order
For
Preliminary Letters
Testamentary**

File No....................

The petition of **Edward Martin** having been filed requesting the issuance of preliminary letters testamentary to **Edward Martin, the Executor named by John Doe in his Will, dated June 10th, 1994,** and the court having entertained the application, and the petitioner having established the necessity for the issuance of such letters, it is

ORDERED that preliminary letters testamentary issue to **Edward Martin**
upon his duly qualifying according to law and upon executing and filing a bond with sufficient surety in the sum of **none;** and it is further

ORDERED that in accordance with the requirements of Section 1412 of the Surrogate's Court Procedure Act, a copy of the petition for preliminary letters testamentary shall be given to each of the persons
whose name and post office address is set forth in paragraph "5" of said petition by personally delivering such copy to such persons or by sending a copy by certified mail to the post office address specified in said petition and filing proof of such personal service or mailing prior to the issuance of the said preliminary letters testamentary; and it is further

ORDERED that *(recite any conditions or provisions as to limitations)*

ENTER:

_____
Surrogate Judge

Appendix F

SOME ALTERNATIVE CLAUSES FOR USE IN YOUR WILL

No two Wills are (or should be) exactly the same, since each person's situation is necessarily unique. Hence, here are a few additional clauses to guide testators in drafting their Wills to suite their individual needs or circumstances.

Giving the Entire Estate to Spouse, with Remainder to Children:

"I hereby give all my property and entire estate, both real and personal, of whatever nature and wherever located, to my wife/husband* *(her/his name?)* , to use during his/her life, and after her/his* death, the same are to go to my children *(their names, addresses)*, their heirs and assigns, in equal shares. If wife (husband) does not survive me, in that event the said estate shall go to my children *(their names, addresses)* , their heirs and assigns, in equal shares."

Trust Provisions in the Event of Death of Spouse Before the Testator:

"I hereby give all my property and entire estate, both real and personal, of whatever nature and wherever located, to my wife (or husband)* *(her name?)* , to use absolutely for herself and the care of our children. If my wife dies before me, I direct that her entitlement herein shall go to Mr./Mrs. *(name of the trustee?)* , who resides at_____ _____, as Trustee, IN TRUST for the following uses and purposes: To hold, invest and manage the said property in trust and without bond or court order, for the benefit of my son, John Doe Jr., and to pay the amounts of income and principal of the said trust which my Trustee considers proper or advisable to my son for his support, education and welfare until he shall attain the age of 25 years when the remaining trust estate shall be distributed to him free of this trust. If my son shall die before receiving final distribution under the trust, I direct that the assets still remaining in the trust be distributed as follows:_____."

Provision to Discourage Contest of the Will:

"In the event that any beneficiary under this Will, or any person whatsoever, shall contest this Will, directly or indirectly, or file, support or be a party to a court action against me, my estate or the executor, about the provisions of this Will, then I direct that the gifts made in this Will or otherwise to such beneficiary shall terminate and become void, and shall revert back to my residuary estate."

OR

"If any person, whether a beneficiary under this Will, or a legal heir of mine, or a person claiming to be a legal heir of mine, shall in any manner either directly or indirectly attack the distribution of my estate or oppose or contest any part of this Will, then and in such event, any gifts to that person or persons provided for in this Will are revoked and that person or persons shall get only the sum of one dollar ($1.00) and no more, or if no gifts are provided for the such person or persons under this Will, then in no event shall that person or persons get more than the said sum of one dollar ($1.00)."

Instructions to Destroy Personal Papers:

"I direct my Executor to carefully examine all my personal papers, letters or other records, and to destroy any or all of them as he may consider too private or personal in his sole judgment."

---

*Enter one or the other.

Marital Deduction Clause:

"I give to my wife, if she survives me, a portion of my estate equal in value to the maximum marital deduction allowable on my estate for the purposes of determining the federal estate tax on my estate, after the value of any property which passes or is considered to have passed to my wife under other provisions of this Will or other instruments, shall have been subtracted in making the said determination of what constitutes my estate."
(NOTE: It should be obvious that this clause would not be appropriate where the entire estate is left to the spouse.)

Leaving Nothing To A Child(or to your parents or brother & sisters, if you have no children):

"I have in mind but have deliberately given nothing to my son, John, for reasons which I consider good and sufficient."

OR

"I have in mind but have deliberately given nothing to my son, John, because I wish to provide for others who are not as well off."

Appointment of an Executor in other states *(applicable mostly to testators with property in several states):*

"If it becomes necessary at any time to appoint an executor or other representative or my estate in any state other than the state in which I am domiciled at the time of my death, I nominate and appoint such person or persons as my Executor then serving may, in his sole discretion, select to serve as my such executor or representative."

Creation of Testamentary Trust

"I give my residuary estate to my spouse, Mr/Mrs_____. If my spouse does not survive me by sixty days and any child of mine under 21 years of age survives me, then I give all my residuary estate to the trustee herein appointed under this Will, in trust, on the following terms:

As long as any child of mine under 21 years of age is living, the trustee shall distribute from time to time, or for the benefit of any one or more of my children and the descendents of any deceased child of any age, as much, or all, of: **(i)** the principal of the trust, or **(ii)** the net income, or **(iii)** both, as the trustee may deem necessary for their health, support, maintenance, and education. Any undistributed income shall be accumulated and added to the principal. "Education" includes, but is not limited to, college, graduate, postgraduate, and vocational studies, and reasonably related living expenses.

I grant my Trustee(s) the full powers and discretion to invest, sell, hire professional help, and otherwise manage and administer the trust assets based on such conditions as the Trustees may deem proper and necessary, all without bond or court order, and always keeping in mind the interest and welfare of the trust beneficiaries.

In furtherance of the Trustee's fiduciary duties, the trustee may distribute trust income or principal in equal or unequal shares and to any one or more of the beneficiaries to the exclusion of the other beneficiaries. In deciding on distributions, the trustee may take into account, so far as known to the trustee, the beneficiaries' other income, outside resources, or sources of support, including the capacity for gainful employment of a beneficiary who has completed his or her education.

On any distribution of assets from the trust, the trustee shall have the discretion to partition, allot, and distribute the assets in kind, including undivided interests in an asset or in any part of it,; or partly in cash and partly in kind; or entirely in cash. If a distribution is being made to more than one beneficiary, the trustee shall have the discretion to distribute assets among them on a pro rata or non pro rata basis, with the assets valued as of the date of the distribution.

The Trust shall terminate when there is no living child of mine under 21 years of age. The trustee shall distribute any remaining principal and accumulated net income of the trust to all my children who are then living, or to their descendents, if they are deceased.

If my spouse does not survive me by sixty days and if no child of mine is under 21 years of age, then I give all my residuary estate to my children in equal shares.

If a trustee is needed to serve under Paragraph ____ of the Will, I hereby appoint _____ to serve."

Appendix **G**

GLOSSARY OF PROBATE AND LEGAL TERMS

Abatement Clause
A clause in a Will by which the Will-maker ensures that in the event he had overestimated the value of his estate, or that it had substantially decreased in value at the time of his death or became smaller than he had anticipated when he made his will and the bequests therein, certain bequests would have preference or priority over others. (Same as Paragraph XII of the Will Practice Worksheets in Chapter 4 of this manual.)

Acknowledgment
A declaration in front of a person who is qualified to administer oaths (such as a Notary Public) that a document bearing your signature was actually signed by you.

Act Of God
An accident which could not have been foreseen or prevented, e.g., those caused by earthquakes, storms, forest fires, and the like.

Ademption
The cancellation of a bequest by reason of some act of the will-maker, such as the subsequent sale of a bequeathed item by the will-maker.

Administration
The conservation, management and distribution of the property (estate) of a dead person.

Administrator
A male person (or a corporation) appointed by a court to manage and settle the estate of a person who died "intestate" — i.e., without leaving a will. The female counterpart is called Administratrix.

Administrator Cum Testamento Annexo
(With the will annexed, abbreviated c.t.a) A person or corporation appointed by a court to manage and settle the estate of a deceased (dead) person who left a will but failed to name an executor in the will; or a person so appointed when the person named in the will fails to qualify or is unable to act.

Affinity
Relationship by marriage. (This contrasts with "consanguinity," which is relationship by blood)

Ancestor
One who precedes another in the line of inheritance (father, mother, grandparents, children, etc., are said to be in "direct" line of ancestry, and uncles, aunts, and cousins, in "collateral" line of ancestry)

Ante-nuptial (Contract)
A contract made by a man and a woman prior to their marriage, in which they detail their property-rights.

Appraisal
A valuation of property; the opinion of an expert as to the true value of real or personal property based on facts and experience.

Appreciation
Increase in value; opposite of depreciation.

Attest
To witness a document in writing, such as the witnessing of the signing of a will.

Attestation Clause
That clause in a will which contains the statement of the persons witnessing the signing of the will; the clause that immediately follows the signature of the will-maker.

Beneficiary One who is the recipient of benefits, such as: 1) the profits or rents of an estate or transaction; or 2) the proceeds of an insurance policy; or 3) the income or profits from a trust fund.

Bequest A gift of personal property by will (Same as Legacy, but contrasts with devise, which is a gift of real property).

Bond A written pledge or obligation, usually issued by a bonding company for a fee, by which the bonding company is to pay a sum of money in case of failure to fulfill an obligation, or of conflicting damages or mishandling of funds

Charitable Bequest A gift of personal property by will to a charity.

Codicil An addition or amendment of a will.

Collateral Incidental; something that is additional to, or an off-shot to a matter. E.g., the term "collateral heir," means a person who falls outside the "direct line" of inheritance, such as a nephew, uncle or aunt.

Community Property The property owned in common or together by husband and wife during their marriage, based on the legal doctrine in certain states that property acquired by either or both parties during marriage belongs to the "marital community."

Competent (Testator or witness). A person who, at the time of his making and signing of his will, had a reasonably sound mental capacity to do so. When used in connection with a witness, the term is generally used to refer to the fitness of the witness to a will to testify credibly in court concerning his role as a witness to the signatory.

Conservator A guardian, protector or preserver.

Corpus Latin word meaning the "body" or principal of an estate, as contrasted with its income or interest.

Curtesy The right of a surviving widower, under an old common law practice, to have an interest in the real property the wife leaves, irrespective of the provisions of her will to the contrary, and irrespective of any debts she might owe, etc.

Death Taxes Same as estate and inheritance taxes.

Decedent The dead person.

Demise 1) Death, decease; 2) To pass by Will or inheritance.

Depreciate To decrease in value; the opposite of appreciate.

Descendant One who descends (proceeds) from the body of another, e.g., a child, grandchild, etc.

Descent The passing on of an estate to another person by inheritance.

Devise A gift of real property by will. The giver is called the devisor, and the person to whom it is given, the devisee.

Direct Heir A person in "direct" line of descent, such as a child or parent.

Distribution Generally, the distribution or apportionment of property or money by an Executor or the court to the heirs or beneficiaries of an estate. More commonly, the term is used to describe a situation where the court distributes the property of a person who dies without leaving a will to those entitled to receive them under the applicable state law. (A "distributee" is one who gets or is entitled to a share in the distribution).

Domicile	One's permanent or legal home, as opposed simply to his temporary place of abode. This differs from a person's "residence" which is used to describe where the person may be living for the time being.
Dower	The right of a surviving widow under an old common law practice, to have an interest in the real property the husband leaves, irrespective of the provisions of his will to the contrary, or any debts he might owe, etc.
Election	The choice of an alternative, such as the right of a widow (or widower) to take the share of her deceased husband's estate to which she is entitled under the law, if she dissents from the provision made in her husband's will..
Encumbrance	A right in real property which, while it diminishes the net value of the property, does not prevent its transfer from one person to another, e.g., liens, outstanding debts or taxes on a house.
Entirety	The phrase "ownership or tenancy by the entirety," is used to describe a situation where two or more persons (but more commonly a husband and wife) jointly own a real property, so that the property cannot be divided up between them. Hence, if one of the parties should die, the whole property goes to the remaining survivor(s).
Escheat	The reversion of property to the state if no heirs or beneficiaries can be found.
Estate	The sum total of the property, both real and personal, owned by a decedent at the time of his death.
Execution	The completion of the making of a document (such as a deed, contract or Will) by officially signing it.
Executor	A male person (or a corporation) named in a Will to see that the terms of the Will are carried out. If a female, she is called an Executrix.
Fiduciary	A general term used to describe a relationship that requires a high trust and confidence. Persons like guardians, trustees, executors and administrators of estates, fall under such a category.
Gift Causa Mortis	A gift of personal property made by a person in contemplation or expectation of death, which is actually delivered by the gift-maker but effective only if the gift-maker dies.
Gift Inter Vivos	A gift of personal property made by a living person to another, which becomes effective only if actually delivered by the gift-maker.
Gift tax	A tax imposed upon the value of a gift.
Guardian	A person who is legally assigned the responsibility of taking care of and managing the property of another person who is incapable of managing his own affairs (e.g., a minor or an incompetent)
Guardian ad Litem	A person assigned by a court to represent a minor or an incompetent while a court action or probate proceedings are pending.
Heir	A person who inherits by virtue of descent or relationship from a deceased person.
Holographic Will	A will written, dated and signed entirely by the will-maker in his own handwriting.
Income	The returns from a property or asset, as opposed to the principal or capital itself (the "corpus"). Rents, interest and dividends are examples of income.
Incompetent	A person who lacks the ability or fitness to understand and manage his own affairs or to discharge the required function.

Infant	A person who is not of the required legal age. (Same as minor)
In Extremis	Something done in extreme circumstance, e.g., the one's last illness.
Inheritance Taxes	A tax assessed on the person who receives a property by inheritance. This tax is based on the recipient's right to receive such a gift, and differs from an "estate" tax, which is assessed on the decedent's estate itself.
Inter Vivos	A trust or gift between living persons; something done during one's liftime.
Intestacy	The state or condition of dying without having made a valid will. One who dies without having left a valid will is said to have died "intestate."
Issues	One's offspring, children or descendents.
Joint Tenancy	The phrase "joint tenancy or joint ownership" is used to describe a situation where two or more persons (usually non-marital partners) own or hold property in joint names, so that if any of them should die, the entire property goes to the remaining survivors. (Nearly the same as "tenancy by the entirety," especially when non-marital partners are involved)
Kin (or Kindred)	Persons related by blood, or with a common ancestry. (Next-of-kin is a person who is next closest relation to a decedent by blood)
Legacy	A gift of personal property by will. (Same as bequest). One who receives or is entitled to receive a personal property under a will is known as a legatee.
Letters Testamentary	A document issued by a court to an executor, by which the said executor is authorized to settle a particular estate.
Lien	A claim on the property of another resulting from some charge or debt.
Mutual Wills	Two separate wills in which each testator (usually a husband and wife) make similar or reciprocal provisions concerning the beneficiaries and executor or executrix.
Natural Guardian	The mother, father or grandparent of a minor.
Non Compos Mentis	Latin for "not of sound mind. Term is used to indicate a state of insanity or intoxication when one has no knowledge of the full meaning or consequences of his act.
Noncupative Will	An oral statement by a person on his death bed or under similar circumstance, as to what should be done with his property, which then becomes the basis of his last will if he should die.
Pecuniary Legacy	A gift of money by will.
Per Capita	Latin, meaning "by the head." When used in wills, it is taken to mean that the property or gift involved should be distributed in equal or share-by-share parts to each of the beneficiaries named.
Per Stirpes	This is the opposite of "Per Capita." When a will-maker makes a gift to a group of beneficiaries 'per stirpes,' it means that if any of the named beneficiaries should die before he could receive the gift, then his children would get, as a class or family, that portion to which their parent would have been entitled if alive.
Perjury	False testimony made under oath.
Personal Property	Any other property other than real property. (Same as personalty)
Posthumus Child	A child born after the father's death.

Principal   The capital of an estate or trust; or the original fund of money or deposit on which interest is paid.

Probate of Will   The formal presentation of the will to a proper court for the purpose of establishing that the will presented is actually the maker's last will.

Pro Se   A person, usually a non-lawyer, who is acting for himself or representing himself in a court case.

Public Administrator   A government official who acts as the administrator of a deceased person's estate when there is no one else named or available or qualified to assume the duty.

Real Property   Land and everything growing or erected on it.

Residuary Estate   The property that is left over in a testator's estate after all the liabilities, bequests and devises are paid out.

Reversion   The return of real property to the original owner or his heirs, after the expiration of a stated period. E.g., when a testator gives a house to his wife for her lifetime only, the house 'reverts' (goes back) to the testator's estate upon the death of the wife.

Revocation of Will   The cancelling or renouncing of an existing will by a subsequent act of the testator, such as making a new will or destroying the old one.

Settlement   The final distribution of an estate by an executor or administrator.

Statutory Share   That portion of a person's property or estate which is allowed to his spouse by the law of the state.

Signature   A signed name or mark on a document to identify the person who made the document.

Subscribe   To write your name yourself, by putting your signature to a written statement or document, such as a will.

Subscribing Witness   One who signed his name on a will as a witness to its execution by the will-maker.

Succession   The state of someone becoming entitled to the property of a deceased person, whether by law or by the provision of a will.

Tenancy by the Entirety   See "Entirety."

Tenancy in Common   The holding of property by two or more persons in such terms that each has an <u>undivided</u> interest in the property, and on the death of one of them, his undivided interest automatically passes to his heirs or devisee(s) and <u>not</u> to the other survivors.

Testamentary Capacity   (Testamentary power). The competency or mental capacity sufficient to make a will.

Testamentary guardian   A guardian named in the will of a decedent.

Testamentary trust   A trust established by the provisions of a will.

Testate   The opposite of intestate; the state of having made or left a valid will at one's death.

Testator   A person (male) who dies leaving a valid will. (Called a testatrix, if a female)

Trust   An obligation upon a person (the "trustee") which arises out of the terms of a special grant, to hold or apply property according to those terms, for the benefit of others (the "beneficiaries").

Verification   Written confirmation of the truth of a document made out and sworn to by a person.

Void   An act or statement which has no legal force, effect or legitimacy from the beginning. (When something is "voidable," it means it has a legal force or legitimacy until and unless someone takes an action that makes it void, or a court declares it so.)

Ward   A person who is under the protection of a guardian.

Widow's allowance   The allowance given to a widow for her immediate needs after the death of her husband.

Appendix **H**

SOME SUGGESTED FURTHER READINGS

A list of readings is included below. They are recommended as possible aids to persons who may, for whatever the objective, want to explore the subject of estate planning and probate, of which Will, Living Will and other related estate planning instruments discussed in this manual, are merely an important integral part.

ALL-STATES WILL & ESTATE PLANNING GUIDE: BASIC PRINCIPLES AND A SUMMARY OF STATE AND TERRITORIAL WILL AND INTESTACY STATUTES. The Editors, Chicago: American Bar Association Section of General Practice, 1990. An excellent overview treatment of the subject.

THE ESSENTIAL GUIDE TO A LIVING WILL, by B.D. Cohen, published by Prentice Hall Press, N.Y. 1991. Book by a Pulitzer-Prize winning reporter, is a competent primer on the subject it addresses.

EVERYTHING YOU'VE ALWAYS WANTED TO KNOW ABOUT THE LAW BUT COULDN'T AFFORD TO ASK, by Edward E. Colby. Published by Major Books, 21335 Roscoe Blvd., Canoga Park, California 91304, and by Drake Publishers, 801 Second Ave., New York, N.Y.

FEDERAL ESTATE AND GIFT TAXES, Revised Sept. 1984—US Internal Revenue Service publication (Publication #448). Revised periodically and available from the IRS Form Distribution Center of your state. Good for reference information on federal estate tax provisions that apply to the estate of individuals dying in 1981 or thereafter.

HANDBOOK OF PROBATE LAW—PRACTICE & PROCEDURE, by Robert 0. Angle. Published by Good Life Press, 658 S. Bonnie Brae St., Los Angeles, California 90057. The price is a little on the upper side, $31.50, but it is a comprehensive work with some important helpful insights for the non-technician.

HOW TO AVOID LAWYERS: A LEGAL GUIDE TO LAYMEN, by Edward Siegel. Published by Fawcett World Library, New York, N.Y.

HOW TO PROBATE, ADMINISTER & SETTLE AN ESTATE YOURSELF WITHOUT THE LAWYERS' FEES , by Benji 0. Anosike, Published by Do-It-Youself Legal Publishers, Newark, NJ. Leads the non-lawyer, step-by-step, through the process of probating and administering an estate without using a lawyer, from start to finish. Complete with specific rules and procedures used for filings in New York and most states; illustrated with sample legal forms.

THE LIVING WILL HANDBOOK, by Alan D. Lieberson, published by Hastings House Book Publishers, Mamaroneck, NY (1991). An excellent and comprehensive guide on the Living Will written by an author who is both a physician and a lawyer.

THE NEW YORK TIMES GUIDE TO MAKING THE NEW TAX LAW WORK FOR YOU, by Karen N. Arenson. Published by Times Books, 3 Park Avenue, N.Y., N.Y. 10016. Explains, in non-technical language, the major aspects of post-1981 tax law, estate and gift tax planning: from tax-saving techniques, to items that are of relevance to a Will-maker from the standpoint of estate taxation.

Other Sources: "Passing On as Much as You Can," in The N.Y. Times, May 30, 1982; "New Unlimited Marital Deduction Changes Estate and Gift Planning," in The N.Y. Times, August 7, 1981, pp. Al & D4; "Estates and Gifts: Planning Simplified," in The New York Times, Sept. 4, 1981, pp. Dl & 4.

Appendix I

ORDERING YOUR BLANK FORMS FOR DRAFTING A WILL, LIVING WILL, AND THE OTHER RELATED DOCUMENTS

For our readers' added convenience, the ***Do-It-Yourself Legal Publishers,*** the nation's original and leading self-help law publisher, makes available to its readership an especially-designed package of forms usable by most for the standard needs. Taken together, the package constitutes the essential forms a planner will need in a "complete" or "total" estate plan scheme (Chapter 1 of the manual). Whether married or single, with children or not, if your situation is uncomplicated and straightforward (as most peoples' situations often are, actually!), you can just as well use these forms for a faster, quicker, but less involved effect.(Or, at least, adapt them to your use accordingly).

The following forms are included in our STANDARD WILL KIT FORMS PACKAGE:

1) The Will

2) The Living Will (General Purpose form), with a "Medical Directive" component

3) Durable Financial & Medical Power of Attorney

4) Affidavit of Agent As To Power of Attorney Being In Full Force

5) Revocation of Living Will and Durable Financial & Medical Power of Attorney

(Customers: For your convenience, just make a zerox copy of this page and send it along with your order. All prices quoted here are subject ot change without notice.) NOTE: Only orders placed by mail will be honored.

TO: **Do-It-Yourself Legal Publishers** (Legal Forms Division)
27 Edgerton Terrace
East Orange, NJ 07017

ORDER FORM

Please send me the publisher's "all-in-one" STANDARD WILL KIT FORMS PACKAGE *[Prices: $29.90 per set]*

FORM	QUANTITY(Sets)	PRICE
For unmarried person WITH minor child(ren)....................................	_____	$ _____
For unmarried person WITHOUT minor child(ren).............................	_____	$ _____
For married person WITH minor child(ren)...	_____	$ _____
For married person WITHOUT minor child(ren).................................	_____	$ _____

(Prices: $29.90 per set)

Subtotal... _____
Postage @ $4 per set .... _____
Sales Tax*... _____
GRAND TOTAL .... $ _____

Answer the following:

My permanent domicile is the city and county of_____, state of_____.

My marital status is_____. I have children: Yes_____ No_____. The child(ren) are: Adults_____ Minors_____

My state provides for a mandatory, state-required Living Will form (see Appendix C): Yes_____ No_____

I bought your book, or read, learned about it from this source (bookstore, library, medium)_____

_____

(Name & address, please)

_____

Enclosed is the sum of $_____ to cover the order, which includes $4 per set for shipping and local sales tax,* as applicable.

Send this order to me:

Mr/Mrs/Ms/Dr._____

Address:_____

City & State:_____ Zip_____ Tel. # (____)_____

*New Jersey residents enclose 6% sales tax.

IMPORTANT: Please do NOT rip out the page. Consider others! Just make a photocopy and send.
And have you please completed our 'Readers Opinion Sheet' on p. 126?

Appendix J

LIST OF OTHER PUBLICATIONS FROM DO-IT-YOURSELF LEGAL PUBLISHERS

Please DO NOT tear our this page. Consider others!

The following is a list of books obtainable from the Do-It-Yourself Publishers/Selfhelper Law Press of America.

(Customers: For your convenience, just make a photocopy of this page and send it along with your order. All prices quoted here are subject to change without notice.)

1. How To Draw Up Your Own Friendly Separation/Property Settlement Agreement With Your Spouse
2. Tenant Smart: How To Win Your Tenants' Legal Rights Without A Lawyer (New York Edition)
3. How To Probate & Settle An Estate Yourself Without The Lawyers' Fees ($35)
4. How To Adopt A Child Without A Lawyer
5. How To Form Your Own Profit/Non-Profit Corporation Without A Lawyer
6. How To Plan Your 'Total' Estate With A Will & Living Will, Without a Lawyer
7. How To Declare Your Personal Bankruptcy Without A Lawyer ($29)
8. How To Buy Or Sell Your Own Home Without A Lawyer or Broker ($29)
9. How To File For Chapter 11 Business Bankruptcy Without A Lawyer ($29)
10. How To Legally Beat The Traffic Ticket Without A Lawyer (forthcoming)
11. How To Settle Your Own Auto Accident Claims Without A Lawyer ($29)
12. How To Obtain Your U.S. Immigration Visa Without A Lawyer ($25)
13. How To Do Your Own Divorce Without A Lawyer [10 Regional State-Specific Volumes] ($35)
14. How To Legally Change Your Name Without A Lawyer
15. How To Properly Plan Your 'Total' Estate With A Living Trust, Without The Lawyers' Fees ($35)
16. Legally Protect Yourself In A Gay/Lesbian Or Non-Marital Relationship With A Cohabitation Agreement
17. Before You Say 'I do' In Marriage Or Co-Habitation, Here's How To First Protect Yourself Legally
18. The National Home Mortgage Escrow Audit Kit (forthcoming) ($15.95)

Prices: Each book, except for those specifically priced otherwise, costs $25, plus $ .00 per book for postage and handling. New Jersey residents please add 6% sales tax. **ALL PRICES ARE SUBJECT TO CHANGE WITHOUT NOTICE**

CUSTOMERS: **Please make and send a zerox copy of this page with your orders)**

ORDER FORM

TO: **Do-it-Yourself Legal Publishers**
27 Edgerton Terrace, East Orange, NJ 07017

Please send me the following:

1._____copies of _____
2._____copies of _____
3._____copies of _____
4._____copies of _____

Enclosed is the sum of $_____ to cover the order. *Mail my order to:*
Mr./Mrs.//Ms/Dr. _____
Address (include Zip Code please): _____
_____
Phone No. and area code: ( ) _____ Job: ( ) _____
*New Jersey residents enclose 6% sales tax.

IMPORTANT: Please do NOT rip out the page. Consider others! Just make a photocopy and send it.

READERS OPINION SHEET

The author (the Publisher as well) is interested in serving **YOU,** the reader, as he's deeply of the view that **YOU,** the consumer, are the KING or QUEEN! He'd love to know: Did this book meet your needs? Did it answer the more general, basic questions that you had; was it to the point? Most importantly, did it get the job done for you—of getting you a good, simple enough Will and other documents? If you would like to express your views directly to the author, ***please complete and return this sheet to:*** *the author,* in care of the Publisher. And we'll make sure your opinion promptly gets directly to him. *Please use the reverse side, if you need extra space.* **[Please do _NOT_ tear out the sheet; just make a photocopy and send that]**

1. The areas *(subject matters, chapters, issues, etc.)* this book covers that were of interest to me were:
    _____
    They were_____ were not_____ covered in sufficient depth.

2. Areas not covered by this book that I would like to see are:_____
    _____

3. The most helpful chapter(s) was (were): 1 2 3 4 5 6 7 8 Appendix A, B, C, D, E, F, G, H

4. The least helpful chapter(s) was (were) 1 2 3 4 5 6 7 8 Appendix A, B, C, D, E, F, G, H

5. The organization of the contents and writing style make the manual easy to read and use? Yes___ No___
    *(Explain/Elaborate:)*_____

6. What did you like best about the book?_____
    _____

7. The concept of do-it-yourself, self-help law you champion is: An excellent idea_____ A bad idea_____
    Why? *(Explain/Elaborate:)*_____

8. How would you improve the manual?_____
    _____

9. My job/profession is:_____

10. I have completed 8-12_____ 13-16_____ over 16_____ years of school.

11. My primary reason for reading this book was:_____

12. I learned about the book through this source or medium:_____

13. The book met my primary need in purchasing the book: Yes_____ No_____

14. It saved me appx. $_____ using the book to get my Will (other documents) drafted without hiring a lawyer.

15. I bought the book, or read it at this bookstore or library *(address in full, please)*_____
    _____

My Name & Address are:_____
_____Zip_____Tel. # (   )_____

Send it to: *Dr. Benji O. Anosike, author• c/o Do-It-Yourself Legal Publishers, "Tell it To The Author" Program,* 27 Edgerton Terrace East Orange, NJ 07017

Index